Copyright ARTFULLY Explained
The Illustrated LEGAL REFERENCE for Visual Artists

Deborah Reid, Esq.
with
Mary Atwood

Copyright © 2024 Deborah Reid

Copyright in Illustrations as noted throughout.

All rights reserved.

First Edition 2024

Ordering Information:

store.bookbaby.com

Authors' Websites:

Reidartlaw.com

MaryAtwoodArt.com

Printed in the USA

Table of Contents

INTRODUCTORY MATERIALS

Disclaimer	8
On Purpose(s)	9
Stories, Picture, Warning Signs and Notes	11
The Order of Things: An Overview	12
Applicable Law	13

THE SUBJECT MATTER OF COPYRIGHT

A Little History	18
The Threshold Requirements	19
That's Original	20
Fix It	22
What You CAN Copyright	25
The Copyrightability of Commercial Works: The Bleistein Principal	26
What You Can NOT Copyright: Other Intellectual Property	28
The Idea/Expression Divide	32
Facts	38
Rewriting History	40
Useful Articles	44
ABC, No ©	47
Geometric Shapes	49
Colors and Coloration	50
Welcome to the Public Domain	52

THE EXCLUSIVE RIGHTS OF COPYRIGHT

Introducing the Bundle of Rights	58
Go Forth and Multiply: Reproduction Rights and Copyright	62
The Right to Make Derivative Works	66
Derivative Works: The Sequel	69
A Few Words About Fan Art and Fan Fiction	70
On Display, Publicly	71
The Performance Right	76
The Distribution Right	79

The First Sale Doctrine	83
Resale Royalties: Not Yet	84
NFTs	85
VARA	86

THE OWNERSHIP OF COPYRIGHT

An Overview of Ownership	90
Who Can Be an Author	91
Collaboration, Co-Authors, Commissions, and Compilations	101
Works Made for Hire	106
Assignments and Transfers	111
Licenses	112
CopyLEFT	115

THE FAIR USE DOCTRINE

A Fair Use Tale	120
Fair Use, the Statute	126
The Four Statutory Factors	127
The First Factor	129
The Second Factor	136
The Third Factor	138
The Fourth Factor	141
All Together Now!	144

THE LEGAL CARE AND PROTECTION OF COPYRIGHT

Giving Your Notice	150
Registration	151
Infringement	158
Cease and Desist!	162
Lawsuits	163
The CASE Act	166
The Digital Millennium Copyright Act	168

To begin.

INTRODUCTORY Materials

What copyright is, why it matters + how this book works.

INTRODUCTORY MATERIALS

Disclaimer

On Purpose(s)
Why We Wrote This Book ♦ The Purpose of Copyright

Stories, Pictures, Warning Signs and Notes

The Order of Things: An Overview

Applicable Law

Copyright Law is Territorial ♦ Copyright and the Constitution ♦ 1st AmendmentISH

Federal Statutes and Treaties ♦ Federal Courts and Cases ♦ The Law is Identical on the Internet

CAVEAT CREATOR or ARTIST BEWARE
DISCLAIMER

This book is intended only as a general discussion of copyright law and concepts.

It is not intended and should not be relied upon as legal advice.

The law changes, and may be different in different places,
and is subject to interpretation by different courts, governments and administrative bodies.

The application of copyright law is very fact specific.

Your use of the information in this book is at your own risk.

It should not be used as a substitute for legal advice.

If you need legal advice, consult with a lawyer.

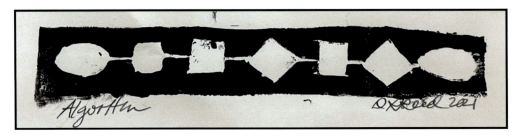

Algorithm by Deborah Reid © 2021

ABOUT LINKS

This book contains links to resources on the Internet to help you find other materials.
We are not responsible for the accuracy of any information provided at these links.
We do not sponsor and are not affiliated or associated with these websites or their creators.

On Purpose(s)

Why We Wrote This Book

Deborah Reid has been practicing law for over forty years. In the early 2000s she was able to practice law less and pick up the paintbrushes she had put down many years before. As she was about to download a local photographer's picture of one of Jacksonville's many bridges she wondered – Is this, okay? She did some legal research and learned that it was not.

Hart of the Night by Mary Atwood © 2021
Isaiah D. Hart Bridge, Jacksonville, Florida

Mary Atwood, an author and accomplished photographer, has had the experience of having other artists tell her that they would like to copy one of her photographs to create a painting. Without Mary's permission it would not be okay. It would be infringement of her copyright.

Our parallel experiences, the burgeoning impact of the technology on visual art, lots of research, many conversations about copyright law and a desire to share our knowledge with our fellow creatives led us, after many twists and turns, to create this book.

The purpose of this book is to educate artists about what a copyright is and what you can and cannot copy - legally - without making your head hurt. You do not need to be a lawyer to understand this subject. As an artist it is wise to do so.

The Purpose of Copyright

The best place to start to understand how copyright works is to appreciate the purpose of copyright. The primary purpose of copyright is the enrichment of public knowledge.

Copyright is a social bargain based on the recognition that creative intellectual activity is vital to the well-being of society. Artists are given monopoly exploitation benefits to incentivize them to share their work with the public.

The public is the intended beneficiary of copyright law. The benefits to artists are secondary considerations.

Copyright law moderates the inevitable tension between the interests of authors in the control and exploitation of their work and the competing interest of society in the free flow of ideas and information.

Public Enrichment by Deborah Reid © 2015

Stories, Pictures, Warning Signs and Notes

We have distilled stories from actual court cases to show how these competing interests have played out over time in the real world.

The stories in this book are drawn from the wellspring of federal copyright case law and include tales of Andy Warhol, Oscar Wilde, and Mitchell Pohl, DDS. Most of the tales are culled from opinions written by federal courts of appeal explaining their answers to pivotal legal questions. The public record often ends at this point. The last chapters of many stories are encased private settlement agreements.

We have created visual explanations of legal concepts, parsed, sliced, and diced statutes and translated legalese into plainer language.

Story by Deborah Reid © 2019

This book will provide you with an overview of the legal landscape, the vocabulary to explore further, and warnings about potential landmines.

We have not used numbered footnotes. The authority for specific statements and links for further research are compiled in the Notes section at the end of this volume.

The Order of Things: An Overview

This book is organized into five main sections. Briefly, these sections cover:

- ***The Subject Matter of Copyright*** – You will learn what types of work are afforded copyright protection. The two threshold requirements of copyrightability, originality and fixation, are explained. The types of work eligible and categorically ineligible for copyright protection are catalogued. The Public Domain is explored.

- ***The Exclusive Rights of Copyright*** – We examine the bundle of exclusive rights conferred on artists for a limited time to allow them to monetize their work. The rights include the right to duplicate the work (quite literally the "copy" right), the right to make derivative works, the rights of public performance and display and the distribution right.

- ***The Ownership of Copyright*** – We introduce you to who can be an author or copyright owner. The specific requirements of Works Made for Hire are explained. You will receive some guidelines to prevent your collaborations from turning into quagmires.

- ***The Fair Use Doctrine*** – Fair use is the right to use copyrighted work without payment or permission in some circumstances. You will learn about the four statutory factors used to analyze fair use. Actual exhibits from actual fair use cases provide some colorful examples.

- ***The Legal Care and Protection of Copyrights*** – Finally, we explain how and why to use copyright notices. You will learn about the important benefits of copyright registration and how to register your work. The legal remedies of infringement lawsuits, DMCA Take Down Notices, and the newly enacted small claims procedures for copyright infringements are summarized.

Copyright Triptych by Deborah Reid © 2022

Applicable Law

Copyright law is dynamic. It evolves in response to both new technology and the social acceptance of different art forms. It responds (sometimes quickly, sometimes slowly) through legislation and judicial interpretation. It rewards the creation of what society values and wants to incentivize at particular times.

Copyright Law is Territorial

Copyright law is "territorial". U.S. law applies to uses of copyrighted material in the United States, regardless of where the work originated. It does not apply to reproductions, distributions, and performances in other countries, or to Internet uses targeted to other countries. In those instances, the law of the country of use may apply and should be consulted.

Copyright and the Constitution

Copyright law in the United States starts with the Copyright Clause of the U.S. Constitution which authorizes the legislature:

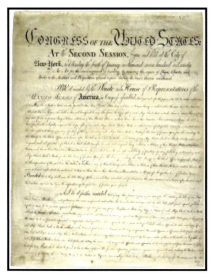

U.S. Constitution

"To promote the progress of science and useful arts, by securing for limited times to authors and inventors the exclusive right to their respective writings and discoveries"

This clause empowers Congress to secure for "authors" exclusive rights in their " writings". Authorship and fixation are *explicit* constitutional requirements for copyrightability, which implicitly presuppose a degree of originality. In other words, writings are what authors created, but for one to be an author the writing has to be original. The definition of writing has expanded from classic literary works to include photographs, sculptures, computer software and blueprints.

1st AmendmentISH

Oddly, the First Amendment of the U.S. Constitution is not technically applicable to copyright. Over the years, efforts to invoke the First Amendment defenses (which would require stricter scrutiny by the Courts and attain wider latitude afforded political speech) have been consistently rejected by the Supreme Court, on the grounds that First Amendment values are already encompassed by the fair use doctrine and the idea/expression dichotomy of copyright law.

Federal Statutes and Treaties

Copyright law in the United States is primarily governed by federal statutes found in Title 17 of the United States Code, a.k.a 17 USC § 101, et seq. The U.S. Copyright Act of 1976, also known as The Digital Millennium Copyright Act and the Visual Artists Rights Act, are all included in Title 17. The U.S. is also party to several international treaties regarding copyright law.

Federal Courts and Cases

The copyright statutes and treaty provisions, where applicable, are interpreted by federal courts, where matters are decided on a case-by-case basis. The written reports of their judicial decisions are referred to as case law.

Lawsuits are initiated and tried in the U.S. District Courts. Appeals from the decisions of these federal trial courts are made to U.S. Circuit Court of Appeals. There are thirteen federal circuits.

The 2nd Circuit Court of Appeals has had profound influence on U.S. Copyright law. New York City, a historic mecca for the theater, television, music, publishing, advertising and other industries with important copyrightable capital, is within its jurisdiction. 2nd Circuit decisions have defined the idea/expression divide and the fair use doctrine.

The 9th Circuit, in which Hollywood and Silicon Valley are located, has also played an important role.

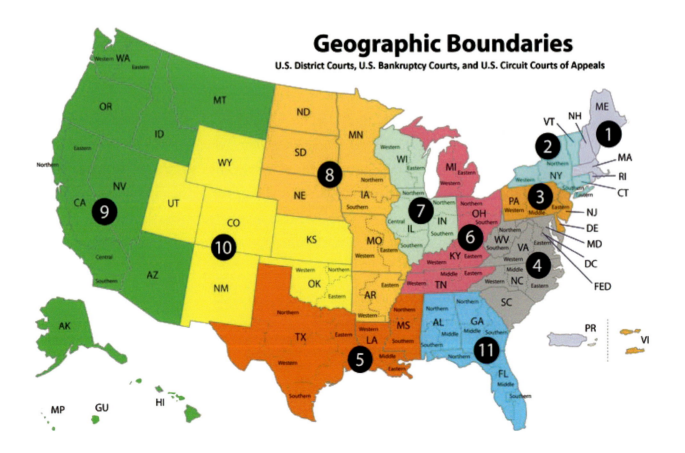

Appeals from the U.S. Circuit Courts of Appeal are made to the U.S. Supreme Court by a writ of certiorari. The Supreme Court only "grants cert", or permission, to a small percentage of cases. Inconsistent decisions between the circuits on an important issue increase the chance of a case being heard by the Supreme Court.

The Law is Identical on the Internet

Copyrights laws apply to online materials in most instances. Many people are under the erroneous assumption that because they can download it, they can legally use it. This is not correct.

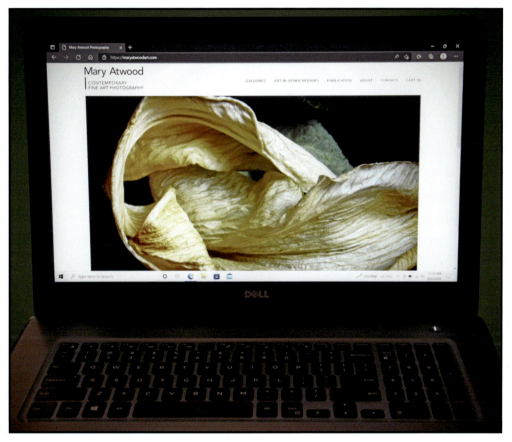

Mary's website on Mary's laptop

The SUBJECT MATTER of Copyright

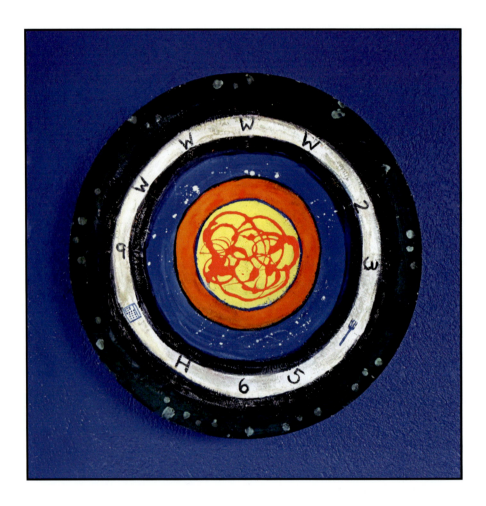

Copyright provides legal protection for original creative expressions.

The Subject Matter of Copyright

A Little History

The Threshold Requirements
Authors + Writings = Originality + Fixation

That's Original
On Photography ♦ Sparks and Bars

Fix It
Fix Your Makeup ♦ The Ephemeral Nature of Nature
A Wet Napkin at the Automat ♦ Fixation is Not Universal ♦ Old World Rules and New Technology

What you CAN Copyright

The Copyrightability of Commercial Works: The Bleistein Principal

What You Can NOT Copyright: Other Intellectual Property
Trademarks: Titles, Slogans, Logos, Symbols, Packaging and Cartoon Characters
Patents: Methods, Inventions, Procedures, Systems, Discoveries, and Some Useful Articles
Trade Secrets

The Idea/Expression Divide
The Law of Ideas ♦ The Starting Line ♦ Some Lines are Drawn ♦ Perspective is Given (or Taken)
Genius is Recognized ♦ The Same Old Story

Facts
Just the Facts ♦ Jellyfish Physiognomy ♦ Dissecting Coqui

Rewriting History
The Empty Chair to the Floor of The Dinner Party ♦ Compilations, Cookbooks, and Cowboys

Useful Articles
Sparrows vs. Canaries

ABC, No ©
Graffiti, Street Art, and Copyright

Geometric Shapes

Colors and Coloration
Paint It Black

Welcome to the Public Domain
The Time Factors ♦ Museum Collections Available ♦ In or Out of the Pool

A Little History

In 1440, Johann Gutenberg invented the printing press. This enabled the rapid mass production of books, and changed the world. Prior to the invention of the printing press there were only few thousand books in existence. There was no such thing as copyright. It simply was not needed. Surreptitious copying was time consuming and arduous. It did not present a problem.

By the year 1500 there were millions of books in Europe alone. In 1710, *An Act for the Encouragement of Learning, by Vesting the Copies of Printed Books in the Authors or Purchasers of Such Copies, During the Times Therein Mentioned* ("Statute of Anne") was enacted in Great Britain in response to this dilemma. It reads, in part:

> "Whereas printers, booksellers, and other persons have of late frequently taken the liberty of printing, reprinting, and publishing, or causing to be printed, reprinted, and published, books and other writings, without the consent of the authors or proprietors of such books and writings, to their very great detriment, and too often to the ruin of them and their families . . ."

Queen Anne and the Statute of Anne

The concept of the public domain was introduced by the Statute of Anne. The public domain, like author and writing, is a term of art. Basically, it means that everything that is not subject to a copyright or the protection of other type of intellectual property is free for anyone to use for anything.

The Threshold Requirements

Authors + Writings = Originality + Fixation

Creative expression is at the core of copyright protection, but not all creative expression is protected by copyright.

A work must first satisfy the threshold requirements of originality and fixation to qualify for copyright protection under U.S. law. These threshold requirements stem from the Copyright Clause of the U.S. Constitution, which empowers Congress to secure for *authors* the exclusive right to their *writings.*

Our Overworked Supreme Court by J. Keppler, 1885

"Author" has been defined by the Supreme Court as "he to whom anything owes its origin; originator; maker; one who completes a work of science or literature." The term author has evolved over the years to include painters, photographers, and software coders. In this book, we use the terms author and artist interchangeably.

The originality requirement has been a constant. It is embodied in the current Copyright Act, which provides copyright protection to "original works of authorship."

"Writings" has been expansively interpreted by the Supreme Court "to include any physical rendering of the fruits of creative intellectual or aesthetic labor." It encompasses, paintings, blueprints, photographs, and computer software. The current Copyright Act provides copyright protection to works of authorship "fixed in a tangible medium of expression."

Not all original works fixed in a tangible medium are eligible for copyright protection. The work must also fall within the scope of copyright protection. Common works included in the subject matter of copyright are literary works, motion pictures, pictorial, and graphic works. Useful articles and ideas are beyond the scope of copyright protection.

That's Original

Copyright protection extends to "original works of authorship". Originality is the *sine qua non* (an essential condition) of copyright.

On Photography

In the 19th century, photography was often perceived as an easier version of painting. Critics described it as a medium that copied everything and explained nothing. This antagonistic attitude influenced the debate over whether copyright protection should be extended to protect photographs. It took decades and a portrait of Oscar Wilde to change this.

In 1884, a young Oscar Wilde travelled to New York to promote a production of *Patience*, a Gilbert & Sullivan operetta, and conduct lectures.

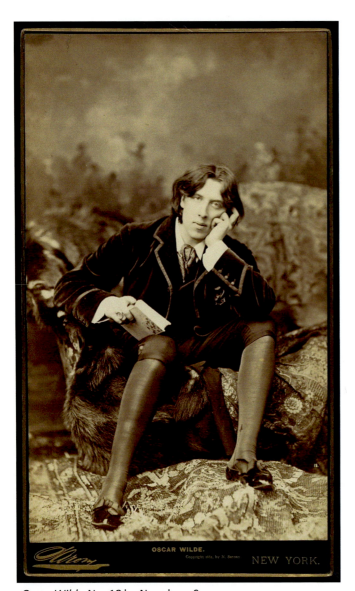

Oscar Wilde No. 18 by Napoleon Sarony

Napoleon Sarony, a successful celebrity photographer, shot a series of publicity photos including *Oscar Wilde No. 18* for Wilde's use on his U.S. tour. Without permission, lithographer Burrows-Giles copied *No. 18* and sold 8,500 copies of it.

When sued by Sarony for copyright infringement, Burrows-Giles defended on the grounds that photographs were "the mere mechanical reproduction of the physical features or outlines of some object, animate or inanimate, and involved no originality or thought". Burrows Giles argued that the authorship and originality required for copyright was lacking.

The Supreme Court found that *No. 18* was a new, harmonious, graceful picture Sarony made from his own mental conception by posing Oscar to present graceful outlines, selecting and arranging the costume, draperies and accessories, using light and shade, and evoking the desired expression. *No. 18* was found worthy of copyright protection.

The view that photography lacks originality has persisted. In 2005, dentist Mitchell A. Pohl routinely took before-and-after photos of his cosmetic dental work for his website. The before-and-after pair of his patient Belinda's dentures went slightly viral and showed up on seven other websites developed by Offcite without Dr. Pohl's permission. Dr. Pohl sued Offcite for copyright infringement.

The trial court ruled that the photos lacked the required originality for copyright protection. The appellate court applied the historically generous standard of originality in evaluating photographs and reversed the ruling.

Elements of originality in a photograph may include posing the subjects, lighting, angle, selection of film and camera, evoking the expression, and almost any other variant. The photographer's copyright is on the photograph itself, not on the subject matter of the photograph. Sarony did not hold a copyright on Oscar Wilde. Dr. Pohl did not get a copyright on the dentures.

Tango by Deborah Reid © 2019

The accurate depiction of Frans Hals' *The Laughing Cavalier* is in the public domain.

Sparks and Bars

For the purposes of copyright law, the bar for originality is low. Novelty, ingenuity, aesthetic or artist merit are not required. Some creative spark no matter how "crude, humble or obvious it might be" will suffice. Although copyright protection is currently afforded to the vast majority of photographs, not all photographs clear the low bar.

Fortunately for artists wishing to reference classical works, there is growing consensus that reproduction photographs which do nothing more than accurately depict works of art in the public domain are not entitled to copyright protection. Although considerable skill may be involved there is simply no independent creation.

Fix It

The Copyright Clause of the U.S. Constitution authorizes Congress to enact legislation to secure for authors exclusive rights in their "writings". Writing is a term of art that has evolved to include photographs, movies, sculptures, musical compositions, and computer software. Works must be "fixed" in a tangible form to be regarded as a "writing" and qualify for copyright protection.

"Fixed" means that a work is sufficiently permanent or stable to permit it to be perceived reproduced or otherwise communicated for more than transitory duration. 17 USC 101. A single work can have multiple fixations. For example, a fictional story can be told in a book, script, screenplay, motion picture or video.

The fixation requirement is easily met by paintings, sculpture, photographs, and other more traditional art forms.

Fixation Trio by Mary Atwood © 2022

The fixation requirement for choreographic works and pantomimes can be satisfied by dance notations such as Labanotation, Benesh Dance Notation, video recordings, textual descriptions, photographs or drawings that reveal the movements in sufficient detail to permit the work to be performed in a consistent and uniform manner. It has also been met by makeup.

Fix Your Makeup

Sammy Mourabit was the makeup artist on a shoot with photographer Steve Klein for *W Magazine*. Klein then partnered with Francisco Nars, another makeup artist, to launch a cosmetic line and used the photographs from the *W* shoot to promote it. Morabito sued for unauthorized use of his makeup artistry.

After determining that makeup artistry was a "pictorial, graphic or sculptural work" the Court rejected the argument that it was not fixed because it is "applied to the face, then photographed (or shown), and removed". A work is fixed when its embodiment is sufficiently permanent or stable to permit it to be perceived, reproduced, or otherwise communicated for a period of more than transitory duration. The few minutes that the makeup was worn was more than sufficient.

The Ephemeral Nature of Nature

Chapman Kelley was a nationally recognized artist known for his romantic floral and woodland scenes set in ellipses. In 1984, the Chicago Park District gave Kelley permission to install two enormous elliptical garden beds planted with a variety of native wildflowers at the north end of Grant Park. "*Wildflower Works*" was described as living art and was greeted with critical and popular acclaim. It was maintained by volunteers.

Standout by Mary Atwood © 2022

The 7th Circuit found *Wildflower Works* was simply too changeable to satisfy the fixation requirement. It queried:

At what point has fixation occurred?

When the garden is newly planted?

When its first blossoms appear?

When it is in full bloom?

* * *

How – and at what point in time –

is a court to determine whether infringing copying has occurred?

The court noted that landscape architects' garden plans reduced to writing, recorded in text, diagrams, drawings done on paper or digitally, were sufficiently permanent and stable to satisfy the fixation requirement. The garden itself, was not.

The Supreme Court declined to hear Kelley's appeal. Chapman Kelley continued to advocate for artist rights even after Wildflower Works was dismantled.

Kelley's fixation issue is not unique. Interesting issues arise in connection with conceptual performances, transitory installations, and fixation.

A Wet Napkin at the Automat

In 1975, Tom Wolfe, the wry, innovative social chronicler described a scenario where the greatest unknown artist in the world dipped his finger into a glass of tap water in a New York City Automat and recorded his greatest inspiration on a paper napkin. Her water strokes diffused and disappeared within seconds. In the 1960s, conceptualists queried whether or not the wetted napkin would have been the greatest work of art ever, or not.

Even if the napkin in the automat was the greatest work of art ever, it likely would not be entitled to copyright protection because of its ephemeral nature. An emphasis on process over product in conceptual and avant-garde art has put some art at odds with the fixation requirement.

Although temporary fixation can be enough to satisfy this threshold requirement, the dynamic transitory nature of improvisation and some performance art pieces will likely be classified as unfixed, and therefore, uncopyrightable. This dilemma is "fixable" (pun intended) simply by recording a transitory work on your phone.

Lost Thoughts by Mary Atwood © 2022

Fixation is Not Universal

While the fixation requirement is firmly embedded in the copyright law of U.S. and common law countries, (where its creation is firmly tied to the invention of printing – a physical medium) it is not a universal requirement of copyright protection internationally. Civil law countries, such as France, Switzerland, Spain, and the Netherlands grant copyright protection once the work is in a form others can perceive. Most Asian nations do not require fixation. In Japan, spoken lectures are protected by copyright. China and Russia also protect oral works.

Old World Rules and New Technology

The awkward application of the fixation requirement to digital technology will be explored further in The Rights of Copyright.

What You CAN Copyright

A work can be protected by copyright if it meets the threshold requirements of originality and fixation AND fits into a category of work within the subject matter of copyright law. Copyright originated and continues to evolve in response to advances in technology.

The types of work that have been allowed copyright protection, in roughly chronological order, include:
- Literary works
- Maps and charts
- Historical and other prints
- Musical works, including any accompanying words
- Dramatic works, including any accompanying music
- Photography and works of art
- Pantomimes and choreographic works
- Pictorial, graphic, and sculptural works
- Motion pictures and other audiovisual works
- Sound recordings
- Computer programs
- Architectural works
- Computer programs
- Vessel hulls

Tools of the Trade by Mary Atwood © 2022

The boundaries of these categories are drawn with broad brush strokes.

The Copyrightability of Commercial Works: The Bleistein Principle

It is well established that works created for commercial purposes are firmly within the subject matter of copyright. Copyright protection extends to fine art masterpieces and mere advertising alike. Critique is not included in the purposes of the court.

Two of the actual posters in question

When asked in 1903 whether works created for commercial purposes should be afforded copyright protection the Supreme Court answered with a resounding "yes". In response to Donaldson Lithographing's claim that its unauthorized use of Bleistein's circus posters was not a copyright infringement because the posters were mere advertising, Justice Oliver Wendell Holmes, writing for the majority, declared:

> "Certainly, works are not the less connected with the fine arts because their pictorial quality attracts the crowd and therefore gives them a real use -- if use means to increase trade and to help to make money. A picture is none the less a picture and none the less a subject of copyright that it is used for an advertisement. And if pictures may be used to advertise soap, or the theatre, or monthly magazines, as they are, they may be used to advertise a circus. Of course, the ballet is as legitimate a subject for illustration as any other. A rule cannot be laid down that would excommunicate the paintings of Degas."

. . . .

> "It would be a dangerous undertaking for persons trained only to the law to constitute themselves final judges of the worth of pictorial illustrations, outside of the narrowest and most obvious limits. At the one extreme some works of genius would be sure to miss appreciation. Their very novelty would make them repulsive until the public had learned the new language in which their author spoke. It may be more than doubted, for instance, whether the etchings of Goya or the paintings of Manet would have been sure of

protection when seen for the first time. At the other end, copyright would be denied to pictures which appealed to a public less educated than the judge. Yet if they command the interest of any public, they have a commercial value -- it would be bold to say that they have not an aesthetic and educational value -- and the taste of any public is not to be treated with contempt."

The judicial refusal to act as an art critic has become known as the Bleistein Principle. This doctrine of avoidance has been employed by U.S. Courts when dealing with the First Amendment issues and National Endowment for the Arts funding cases as well as copyright law.

Under the Big Top by Mary Atwood © 2018

What You Can NOT Copyright: Other Intellectual Property

Legend has it that when Michangelo was asked how he created his masterpiece sculpture *David*, he replied that he simply chipped away the marble that did not look like *David*. To illustrate the subject matter of copyright we are going to chip away what it is not.

Universe of Intellectual Property by Deborah Reid © 2016

Intellectual property law is a loose group of legal doctrines that regulate the use of ideas, images, information, and symbols. It includes copyright, trademark, patent, and trade secret law. The rights of publicity and privacy are closely related. In the U.S., all of these bodies of law are influenced by the First Amendment.

Copyright is the form of intellectual property that protects original artistic expression. However, all kinds of expression are not eligible for copyright protection. Titles, slogans, mottos, methods, procedures, systems, U.S. government publications, utilitarian objects, lists of ingredients, plots, themes, the alphabet and typefaces, facts, and ideas are categorically ineligible for copyright protection. Some of these can be protected by trademark, patents, or trade secret law. Others, not at all.

Trademarks: Titles, Mottos, Slogans, Logos, Symbols, Packaging and Cartoon Characters

Trademark law provides protection for titles, mottos, slogans, symbols, logos, and packaging used to brand goods and services for consumers. Trademark law can also provide protection for cartoon characters if the character functions as a brand identification. Think Mickey Mouse.

If a trademark is in continuous use its protection can be extended indefinitely. One of the oldest trademarks still in use in the United States is the Underwood Deviled Ham Spread trademark, which was registered in November of 1870. Internationally, Stella Artois is said to have been using the same mark since 1366, and Löwenbräu began using their lion trademark in 1383.

Symbol: Logo   **Motto: Slogan**   **Packaging: Trade Dress**

Trademarks do not provide universal monopolies on the use of a words or phrases in every context. The key to obtaining trademark protection for titles, mottos, slogans, colors or design elements is use in connection with particular goods and services.

For example, Tiffany does not have a monopoly on the use of robin's egg blue in the universe or even just New York City. It can only prevent its use where an ordinary consumer is likely to assume that the color means that the goods originated from Tiffany's. Anyone is entitled to make a robin's egg blue bicycle, but a robin's egg blue box with a white ribbon to package jewelry would be problematic.

Tiffany's robin's egg blue packaging is a prime example of trade dress. Trade dress is a term of art that generally refers to characteristics of the visual appearance of a product, or its packaging, that signify the source of the product to consumers. It can include size, shape, color, texture and graphics.

Patents: Methods, Inventions, Procedures, Systems, Discoveries, and Some Useful Articles

Patent law protects some methods, inventions, procedures, systems, discoveries, and some useful articles. Like copyright, patents are a social bargain. In exchange for disclosure of information that would allow others to practice the invention, patent owners are given the exclusive right to use the invention for a maximum term of 20 years. The bar to obtain a patent is high.

There are three kinds of patents: utility, design, and plant patents. Utility patents protect the way an article is used and works. Design patent protects the way an article looks. Plant patents protect the invention or discovery and asexual reproduction of a new variety of plant.

Design patents are often referred to as industrial design outside the United States. Design patent coverage may overlap with copyright and trade dress protection. Smartphones and automobiles are good examples of overlapping coverage.

Trade Secrets

Trade secret law provides protection for methods, products and processes that are not eligible for copyright or other intellectual property protection. A trade secret is information that derives value from not being known by others. For example, a particular way in which paint is mixed or a photograph is developed could be trade secrets; if in fact, they are kept secret.

Shhh by Mary Atwood © 2020

While unauthorized acquisition of a trade secret can be remedied by a suit for misappropriation in most states, a trade secret owner does not have the right to prevent others from developing the same information independently.

Unlike copyrights and patents, trade secrets can last forever. Coca Cola was invented in 1892. If Coke had obtained a patent, it would have expired over 100 years ago and the formula would have been available for anyone to use. It is still a secret.

The most important way to protect a trade secret is to keep it secret. You can use Non-Disclosure Agreements with assistants, collaborators, or employees. More importantly, use common sense. You can have the best written protection in place, but if you are chatting about it in Starbucks you are not keeping it secret. Don't talk, tweet or blog about it. In three words: Keep it secret.

Pause by Deborah Reid © 2020

THE IDEA/EXPRESSION DIVIDE

Idea Expression Divide Diptych by Deborah Reid © 2018

IDEA	EXPRESSION
Concept. Conception. Thought. Theory. Notion.	Articulation. Formulation. Interpretation.
Doctrine. Design. Scheme. Hypothesis.	Execution. Elucidation. Exposition. Rendition.
Essence. Brainstorm. Flash.	Declaration. Narration. Utterance. Locution. Voice.

DIVIDE

Separation. Segregation. Demarcation. Dichotomy. Partition.

The Idea/Expression Divide

The Law of Ideas

Copyrights do not protect ideas. Only the expression of an idea, and not the idea itself, is protectable by copyright.

Ideas are as "free as the air".

Every idea, theory, and fact in a copyrighted work is instantly available for public exploitation at the moment of publication. An author's copyright monopoly extends only to the particular tangible form in which the author expressed the idea.

Everyone else is free to be inspired by the same idea and express it in their own way.

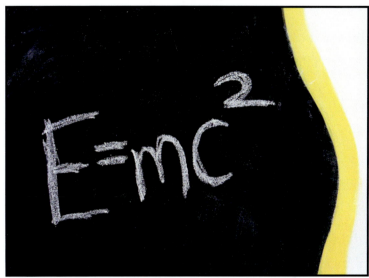

Relativity by Deborah Reid © 2018

This is the idea/expression divide (a.k.a. the idea/expression dichotomy). It is an effort to reconcile the competing societal interests of rewarding individual ingenuity and fostering further improvements from others' use of the same subject matter.

Where to draw the line between an unprotectable idea and a protectable expression is less than clear. The distinction between an idea and its expression is elusive and often an impenetrable inquiry. It is particularly intangible when artistic sensibilities are involved.

The legal landscape is summed up in the oft repeated maxim:

"No one has ever been able to fix that boundary, and nobody ever can."

~Learned Hand in *Nichols v. Universal Pictures*

Think About It, Rodin by Mary Atwood © 2013

The Starting Line

The origin story for the idea/expression divide in the United States has its roots in the "fine art" of accounting.

There are "No Bright Lines" or clear boundaries to be found in the Idea/Expression Divide territory. There are a few case stories which shed light on its contours.

The seminal U.S. case is *Baker v. Selden.* Charles Selden devised a bookkeeping system that produced the same results as a double entry system, but could be presented in less space. *Selden's Condensed Ledger,* or *Book-keeping Simplified*, was published in 1859. It included an introductory explanation of his system with annexed blank forms with ruled lines and headings illustrating the system and its use. Selden registered the copyright for the book, and his two subsequent books which added to his peculiar system.

Blurry by Deborah Reid © 2019

When Baker published account books using substantially the same system, Selden sued for copyright infringement. The matter made its way to the Supreme Court, which agreed with Baker's defense that the "matter alleged to be infringed is not a lawful subject of copyright."

In a landmark decision, the Supreme Court analogized Selden's explanation of his accounting system to copyrighted treatises on the use of medicine, the mixture and application of colors for painting or dyeing, or the mode of drawing lines to produce the effect of perspective. All could be copyrighted, but none would have the exclusive right to use the methods explained. The purpose of publishing such books – and the purpose of copyright – is communication of useful information to others.

A copyright could not prevent anyone from using the method Selden explained, it only prevented the use of his explanation.

Some Lines are Drawn

The Supreme Court compared the ruled lines and headings of the annexed forms to lines a bookkeeper would make with his pen or a stationer with a press. The lines were seen as no more than mere language to convey Selden's ideas more clearly and could not prevent his system or ideas from being used by others.

Absent by Mary Atwood © 2013

Perspective is Given (or Taken)

The Court explained that the copyright of a book on perspective, no matter how many drawings or illustrations it contained, would not give the book's author an exclusive right to use the method of drawing described, even if it had never been known or used before. The author could only prevent others from using his particular expression, i.e., the actual drawings included in his book.

Genius is Recognized

The Supreme Court went on to say:

> "Of course, these observations are not meant to apply to ornamental designs, or pictorial illustrations addressed to the taste . Of these it may be said, that their form is their essence, and their object, the production of pleasure in contemplation. This is their final end. They are as much the product of genius and the result of composition, as are the lines of the poet or the historian's periods."

To further illustrate the concept of the idea/expression divide, let's take a look at some illustrations from actual cases.

Don't Jump

Kaplan v Stock Market Photo Agency, 133 F. Supp2d 317 (SDNY 2001)
Kaplan alleged that the photo (below right) infringed his photo (below left). He lost.

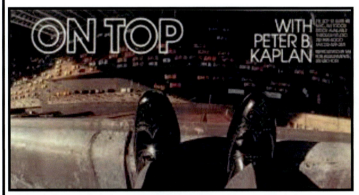

Wing Tips Over the Edge by Peter B. Kaplan

Stock Market Image

A businessman perched on the ledge of a tall building looking down as if contemplating suicide is the central idea of both photos and is a non-copyrightable idea. The vantage point and attire flow naturally from the idea, and are also non-copyrightable. The copyrightable elements (background, lighting, shading, and color) were not similar.

RULING: NO INFRINGEMENT

Watch the Cat and Mouse

Direct Marketing of Va, v. E.Mishan & Sons, Inc. 753 F. Supp 100 (SDNY 1990)

Direct Marketing product

Likely infringement

The *idea* of a watch face with a full-bodied cat which appears to 'see' a mouse as the mouse circles the cat in the manner of a second hand is an unprotectible idea.

Use of America's favorite cat, the Tabby' in a sitting position facing to the left with a stylized rather than realistic rendering of a mouse likely crossed the line and copied Direct Marketing of Virginia.

RULING: INFRINGEMENT

Manhattan Mohawk

Kerr v. New Yorker Magazine, 63 F. Supp. 2d 320 (SDNY 1990)

The similarity between the works is limited to the unprotectible idea of a Manhattan skyline mohawk haircut.

The two figures have an entirely different "concept and feel." Kerr's pen and ink drawing has a sketchy, edgy feel to it, while Kunz's cool colors and smooth lines gives a more serene and thoughtful impression. The idea may be the same, but it is expressed differently.

RULING: NO INFRINGEMENT

New York Hairline by Thomas Kerr

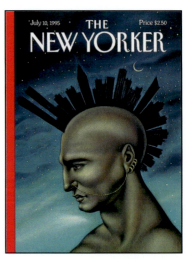

Mohawk Manhattan by Anita Kunz

The Same Old Story

"*Scènes à faire*" are sequences of events that necessarily flow from the choice of a setting or situation, rather than from an author's creativity. Fables, folk lore, boy meets girl, star crossed lover story lines, stock images, visual and cultural references are all stories which must, and have, been told. *Scènes à faire* are in the public domain and are not copyrightable.

Mary and Her Mother *Deborah and Her Mother*

My Mother is the Most Beautiful Woman in the World, by Rebecca Rehyer, was based on a story told to her as child about a young girl who was separated from her family during harvest season in the Ukraine. Wheat harvesting, elaborate costumes, and the feast are described in vivid detail. The lost girl describes her mother as the most beautiful woman in the world to a group of unfamiliar villagers trying to help find her. When the villagers assemble all the women they consider to be beautiful, the mother is not among them. The girl's mother, seen as homely by the villagers, arrives and is joyfully reunited with her child. The village leader declared, "We do not love people because they are beautiful, but they seem beautiful to us because we love them."

When Sesame Street later aired a skit and published a two-page story in its magazine titled *The Most Beautiful Woman in the World,* Reyher sued for copyright infringement.

The Sesame Street piece opens with a little boy crying in the fields because he has been separated from his mother. Thatched huts and people in African tribal dress populate the illustrations. The little boy also describes his mother as the most beautiful woman in the world. Again, when all the local beauties are assembled, the mother is not among them. When the mother arrives on the scene she is seen as old and unattractive by the others, prompting the village leader to declare "what's not so beautiful to some can be very, very beautiful to others."

The common elements: a lost child, a mother's familiar face as the most beautiful face, difficulty finding the mother because of the "most beautiful face" description were scenes which necessarily develop from identical situations. The theme was uncopyrightable as a *scène à faire*. There was no infringement because Sesame Street did not utilize the concrete details of Ukrainian harvests.

Facts

Facts by Deborah Reid © 2022

Just the Facts

- Facts exist and are not created.
- Discovering a fact is not the same thing as creating a work.
- The first person to find and report a particular fact has not created the fact; he or she has merely discovered its existence.
- Facts, like ideas, once revealed are free for all to copy at will.
- Facts are not copyrightable because they are not original.
- Facts are in the public domain.
- This is not unfair or unfortunate. It is the means by which copyright advances the progress of science.
- The original way a fact is expressed may be copyrightable.
- Copyright protection extends to original works of authorship.
- Originality requires independent creation and minimal degree of creativity.

Jellyfish Physiognomy

Richard Satava created a successful line of glass-in-glass jellyfish sculptures. When Christopher Lowry created a glass-in-glass jellyfish sculpture, Satava sued for copyright infringement.

The objective facts of jellyfish such as tendril-like tentacles, rounded bells, bright colors and vertical swimming were not original and not copyrightable. Use of a glass-in-glass structure to showcase an aquatic animal was also not original. These elements of Satava's work were in the public domain and free for anyone to use.

The distinctive curls of particular tendrils, the unique shape of the bells and arrangement of certain hues were original, copyrightable, and afforded Satava "thin" copyright protection. In other words, Satava could copyright his original embellishment of jelly fish, but not his depiction of the actual jellyfish physiognomy.

Dissecting Coqui

The coqui is a tree frog indigenous to Puerto Rico. Coquico, Inc. sued Angel Edgardo Rodriguez-Miranda and Indentiko, Inc. for copyright infringement of its plush toy coqui with a Puerto Rican flag on its underbelly.

The court explained that Coquico could not assert a monopoly on depiction of real coqui features like two eyes, two ear discs, four legs, four front toes and five rear toes. The distinctive stitching pattern, idiosyncratic color combination, flag placement and dimensions were all copyrightable and copied by defendants who were held liable for copyright infringement.

Feeling Froggy by Mary Atwood © 2010

Rewriting History

Copyright protection has never extended to history, whether it is a documented fact or an explanatory hypothesis. The cause of knowledge is best served when history is the common property of all, and each generation remains free to draw upon the discoveries and insights of the past.

Copyright protection for historical accounts extends only to an author's original expression. The facts revealed or theories unveiled are already in the public domain. Absent the wholesale usurpation of another's expression, copyright infringement lawsuits where works of history are at issue are rarely successful.

The evolution of Anna Ella Carroll's story is a good example.

The Empty Chair to the Floor of The Dinner Party

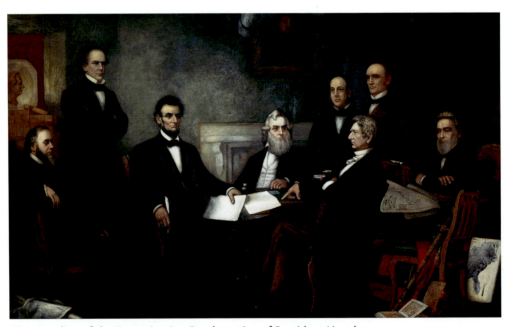

First Reading of the Emancipation Proclamation of President Lincoln
by Frances Bicknell Carpenter, 1864

In 1940 Marjorie Barstow Greenbie's *My Dear Lady, The Story of Anna Ella Carroll, A Great Unrecognized Member of Lincoln's Cabinet* was published. *My Dear Lady* is a historical account of the background, childhood, and Civil War activities of Anna Ella Carroll. Anna was a member of a prominent political family and became a pamphleteer and unofficial member of President Lincoln's cabinet. She is often credited (or not) for the "Tennessee Plan" campaign in the Civil War. It has been reported that the plan was not attributed to her at the time because no one would want to follow a plan conceived by a civilian or a woman. Many view the empty chair in the official painting above as a reference to Anna.

In 1948 *Lady with a Sword,* a fictionalized account of Anna Ella Carroll's career by Hollister Noble, was published. All of the characters in this tome, with one exception, were real people. The basic narratives of both books were predicated on historical facts, or reasonable inferences based on those facts, and followed the chronology of the actual military and political events involved. Marjorie Greenbie filed suit against Noble claiming copyright infringement.

Marjorie Greenbie's claim for copyright infringement was rejected. The court explained that one cannot build a story around a historical incident and then claim exclusive right to the use of the incident. If originality could be claimed by the first story about "then all the novels, short stories, and dramas written about the Civil War, opposing Grant and Lee, might never have been written after the first one because the author of the first one could have claimed exclusive right to the product."

Carroll's story has since been told and retold. Her biography in official Archives of Maryland reports:

> "Carroll's work went mostly unrecognized during her lifetime. As the women's suffrage and women's rights movements gained strength in the later nineteenth and early twentieth centuries, however, the lack of recognition Carroll received during her career was looked at as a "symbol of male injustice," and Carroll herself became a model of a woman who had accomplished significant work in male-dominated areas. Whatever the truth may be regarding her role in the formulation of the Tennessee Plan, it is unquestionable that she served in capacities that went beyond the traditional role of women."

Anna Ella Carroll's name is inscribed on a tile on the Heritage Floor of Judy Chicago's *The Dinner Party* installation at Elizabeth A. Sackler Center for Feminist Art at the Brooklyn Museum. The legend for Anna Ella Carroll in this exhibit characterizes Carroll as a relentless self-promoter from a slave-owning family who "disliked' slavery but condemned the Emancipation Proclamation.

These evolving views illustrate the contrast between these two treatments and illustrate the important First Amendment values served by excluding facts from the protection of copyright. Sometimes history needs to be rewritten.

Compilations, Cookbooks, and Cowboys

A compilation is a work "formed by the collection and assembling of preexisting materials, or of data that are selected, coordinated, or arranged in such a way that the resulting work as a whole constitutes an original work of authorship."

The term "compilation" includes collective works. A compilation copyright protects the order and manner of the presentation of the compilation's elements, but does not necessarily embrace the actual elements themselves.

Facts, whether alone or as part of a compilation, are not original and therefore may not be copyrighted. A factual compilation is eligible for copyright if it features an original selection or arrangement of facts, but the copyright is limited to the particular selection or arrangement. In no event may copyrights extend to the facts themselves.

Discovering Dannon by Mary Atwood © 2023

Like facts, ideas, procedures, and processes are not protectible by copyright. As shown by the Meredith case below, this can foreclose copyright protection for recipes in several ways: as an idea of something to cook, as a statement of facts of what to include, and as a procedure or process of how to make it.

Meredith Corporation published magazines and books of cooking recipes featured for sale at checkout stations in supermarkets. Its *Discover Dannon- 50 Fabulous Recipes with Yogurt* included "Simple Snacks, Exciting Entrees and Dazzling Desserts". Meredith discovered that Publications International had copied and included *Discover Dannon* recipes in twelve of its competing publications and sued for copyright infringement.

The *Discover Dannon* recipes consisted of lists of required ingredients and directions for combining them to achieve the final products. There were no creative narrative or expressive elaborations on the functional components. The 7th Circuit found that the author of "Curried Turkey and Peanut Salad" was not giving expression to individual creative labors, but was writing down an idea. It classified the list of ingredients as a statement of facts and the directions as a procedure, process, or system excluded from copyright protection.

Meredith fashioned processes for producing appetizers, salads, entrees, and desserts. Although the inventions of "Swiss 'n' Cheddar Cheeseballs" and "Mediterranean Meatball Salad" were at some time original, there can be no monopoly (in the copyright sense) for the ideas for producing certain foodstuffs. Nor can there be copyright in the method one might use in preparing and combining the necessary ingredients. Protection for ideas or processes is the purview of patent.

Recipes that contain creative expression in addition to lists and instructions may qualify for limited copyright protection.

Judy Barbour is "the rootin'-tootin' author of *Cowboy Chow*, a Texas-themed cookbook 'containin' larapin' recipes, 'entertainin' ideas', historical information, and other cowboy fun." When Texas Online, an Internet magazine, published *Cowboy Chow* recipes, virtually and verbatim without permission, Barbour sued. In response, Texas Online referenced the Meredith case and requested judgement in its favor.

The trial court denied Texas Online's request. It found that some recipes contained statements that may exceed the boundaries of mere fact.

Yee Haw by Mary Atwood © 2022

Unlike the *Discover Dannon* recipes, *Cowboy Chow* recipes were infused with light-hearted or helpful commentary, parenthetically. The Cherokee Chicken recipe stated: "Heat oil in heavy skillet. Add sugar and let it brown and bubble. (This is the secret to the unique taste!)". "Crazy Horse Cranberry Sauce with Raisins," stated ("Great with all your meats!"). The parenthetical morsels were copyrightable.

Useful Articles

Teapots, wheels, whisks, wrenches and pencils are all useful, and all uncopyrightable. A "useful article" is an item which has an intrinsic utilitarian function that is not merely to portray the appearance of the article or to convey information. Parts of useful articles, like spouts, spokes and handles are also considered to be useful articles. Useful articles (a.k.a. utilitarian objects) are categorically ineligible for copyright protection.

Pictorial, graphic, or sculptural features of useful articles are eligible for copyright protection if those features "can be identified separately from, and are capable of existing independently of, the utilitarian aspects of the article."

The Supreme Court case *Mazer v. Stein* shines some light on this. Stein sculpted a series of Balinese and Egyptian dancers and then made production molds for casting copies. The statuettes were registered with the U.S. Copyright Office as "works of art". The statuettes were manufactured and sold by Reglor as statuettes as well as base components of fully equipped lamps.

Useful Things by Deborah Reid © 2019

Mazer, a self-described manufacturer of human action lamps, removed the copyright notice, copied the statuettes, embodied them into their own lamps and sold them.

A flurry of litigation ensued in federal courts throughout the United States. Mazer's argument that Stein's copyrights were invalid because the statuettes were incorporated into useful articles within the realm of design-patent protection yielded varying results. The Supreme Court reviewed the matters, and cleared up the inconsistency.

The Supreme Court held that the patentability of the statuettes, fitted as lamps or unfitted, does not preclude copyright protection for works of art. Some works, such as the sculpted dancers produced by Stein, can be protected by both copyrights and design patents.

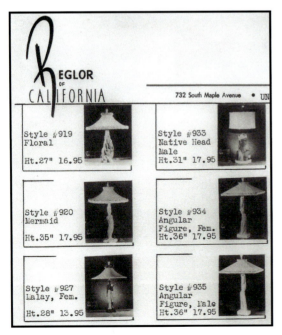

Some of the lamps from *Mazer v. Stein*

Over the years, the standard laid out in *Mazer* mutated.

In 2016, the Supreme Court stepped in, again, to clear up inconsistencies between the circuits as to the copyrightability of utilitarian objects.

Varsity Brands registered two-dimensional designs consisting of lines, chevrons, and colorful shapes appearing on the surface of cheerleading uniforms with the U.S. Copyright Office. Varsity sued Star Athletica, another uniform manufacturer who used the same designs on their own uniforms, for copyright infringement.

The Supreme Court found that the pictorial and graphic qualities were stand alone, two-dimensional works of art. In rejecting Star Athletica's argument that designs were not copyrightable because the shape of the uniform would be retained even after the designs were extracted from them, the Supremes explained:

> "Just as two-dimensional fine art corresponds to the shape of the canvas on which it is painted, two-dimensional applied art correlates to the contours of the article on which it is applied. A fresco painted on a wall, ceiling panel, or dome would not lose copyright protection, for example, simply because it was designed to track the dimensions of the surface on which it was painted."

Varsity designs registered with the U.S. Copyright Office | *Varsity Brands and Star Athletica Designs*

To be clear, the only feature of the cheerleading uniform eligible for copyright protection was the two-dimensional work of art fixed in the tangible medium of the uniform fabric – the surface decorations. The court ruled on appeal that Varsity does not have a right to prohibit any person from manufacturing a cheerleading uniform of identical shape, cut, and dimension - minus the surface decorations.

In sum, an artistic feature of a useful article is eligible for copyright protection if the feature:

- can be perceived as a two or three-dimensional work of art separate from the useful article (the separate identification requirement) and
- would qualify as a protectable pictorial, graphic or sculptural work either on its own or in some other medium if imagined separately from the useful article (the independent existence requirement).

Sparrows vs. Canaries

Design Ideas, Ltd. registered a copyright for Sparrow Clips; clothespins with a colorful silhouetted bird on top. When Meijer, Inc. sold the Canary Clips shown at left without its authorization, Design Ideas sued. Meijer argued that Sparrow Clips were utilitarian objects ineligible for copyright protection.

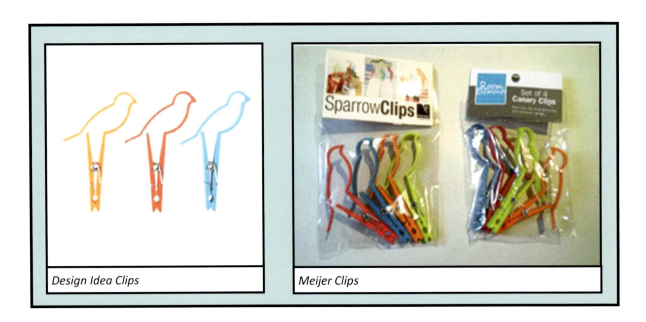

Design Idea Clips | *Meijer Clips*

Using the Star Athletica test, the court held that the bird portion of the Sparrow Clips is subject to copyright protection. First, the bird portion can be perceived as a three-dimensional work of art separate from the useful article. The bird portion has pictorial, graphic, or sculptural qualities. Second, the bird portion would qualify as a protectable sculptural work on its own if imagined separately from the useful article into which it is incorporated. The bird portion would be eligible for copyright protection as a pictorial, graphic, or sculptural work had it been originally fixed in some tangible medium other than attached to the clothespin. "A sculpture does not become a useful article simply because it could be used as a doorstop or a paperweight."

ABC, No ©

Alphabets are the building blocks of languages. Alphabets are quintessentially useful. Alphabets, letters, and words are not copyrightable. The ABCs are in the public domain and are free for all to use. So are standard symbols like # * % © and !.

Typeface, typefont, lettering, calligraphy, and typographic ornamentation are classified as mere variations of uncopyrightable letters and words.

The Copyright Office typically refuses to register claims based on alphabetic, numbering characters, sets or fonts of related characters, fanciful lettering, calligraphy, and other forms of typeface except in very limited instances.

ABC, No © by Deborah Reid © 2023

For example, a representation of an oak tree, a rose, or a giraffe that forms the entire body or shape of a typeface character may be copyrightable. Flourishes, swirls, vector ornaments, scrollwork, and other add-ons to the character may be separately copyrightable just like the graphics separable from the cheerleading uniforms in *Star Athletica, L.L.C., v. Varsity Brands, Inc.*

The source codes of computer programs that generate or use typeface and typefont designs are copyrightable. In this instance, the copyright protects the source code only, not the lettering, fonts, or typeface generated. The use of these programs is governed by End Use Licensing Agreements (EULA).

Graffiti, Street Art, and Copyright

Graffiti (derived from the Latin *graphein,* meaning to write) has been around since the Roman Empire, at least. Graffiti limited to tags, letters, words, and simple phrases is uncopyrightable.

The term graffiti is now widely used to refer to an artistic movement associated with 20th century urban environments. This broad reference encompasses street art. Street art is often image based and is painted with permission. Street art is clearly copyrightable.

More narrowly, graffiti refers to art that has been illegally fixed to property. There is no definitive answer as to whether graffiti's illegality makes it ineligible for copyright protection. Numerous lawsuits involving the fashion industry's use of copying graffiti without permission of the graffiti artist were settled by the parties before the issue was ruled on by the courts. Commentators often side with the graffiti artists in favor of copyrightability.

Everything is Possible by Mary Atwood © 2013

Geometric Shapes

Common geometric shapes such as straight or curved lines, circles, ovals, spheres, triangles, cones, squares, cubes, rectangles, diamonds, trapezoids, parallelograms, pentagons, hexagons, heptagons, octagons, and decagons, either in 2D or 3D form are not copyrightable.

Here are some illustrations constructed from text description examples in the Compendium of the U.S. Copyright Offices Practices:

A standard pentagon with no additional design elements.
NOT COPYRIGHTABLE

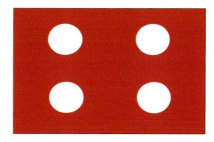

A red background and evenly spaced white circles; does not contain a sufficient amount of creative expression.
NOT COPYRIGHTABLE

A marble sphere; common shape and design in marble is a natural element.
NOT COPYRIGHTABLE

Artwork that merely consists of common geometric shapes is not copyrightable unless the work as a whole is sufficiently creative.

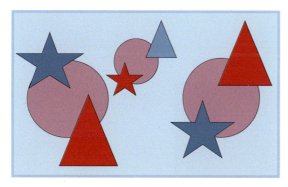

A wrapping paper design that includes circles, triangles, and stars arranged in an unusual pattern with elements portrayed in different colors. Exhibits a creative design that goes beyond the mere display of a few geometric shapes in a preordained or obvious arrangement.
COPYRIGHTABLE

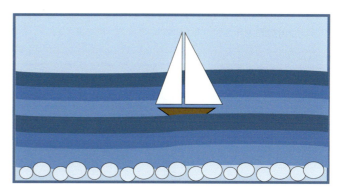

A painting of a beach scene that includes circles of varying sizes representing bubbles, striated lines representing ocean currents, as well as triangles representing sails. Exhibits a creative design that goes beyond the mere display of a few geometric shapes in a preordained or obvious arrangement.
COPYRIGHTABLE

Colors and Coloration

You can NOT copyright a color.

You may be able to obtain a trademark for use of a color in connection with particular goods or services. Tiffany has the trademark on tiffany blue for use on jewelry boxes and packaging. UPS has the trademark on brown for use with courier services.

Coloration or variations in coloring alone, even when the result is unexpected, or more aesthetically pleasing are not copyrightable. This is true if the changes are made by hand, computer or other process. The colorization of old black and white movies was not copyrightable.

Here are some examples straight from the Copyright Compendium:

NOT Copyrightable

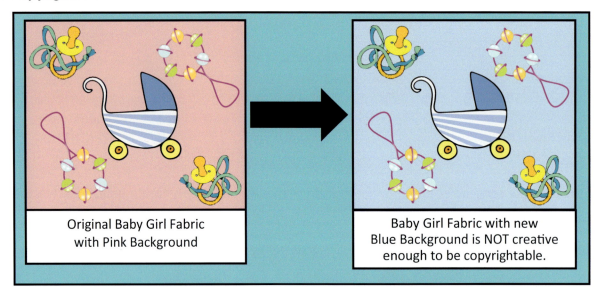

MAYBE/MAYBE NOT

Watercolor World by Mary Atwood © 2022

The copyrightability of adding colors to someone else's coloring book depends on whether it was sufficiently creative.

YES Copyrightable (Creative) Coloring

Photograph digitally edited to add new shades of blue and red in certain places; the creativity in the photograph, together with the alteration of the colors, is sufficiently creative.

Paint it Black

Vantablack, " the blackest black" paint was invented by Surrey Nanosystems for military purposes. Artist Anish Kapoor believed in its artistic potential and secured a license from Surrey for its exclusive use in painting and sculpture.

Anish Kapoor's possible monopoly on the use of the blackest black paint was not because he has a copyright. He does not. If he does have a monopoly, it is because of his agreement with Surrey NanoSystems, the manufacturer of Vantablack.

Vantablack may no longer be the blackest black. In response to Aneesh Kapoor's black deal, another manufacturer, NanoLab, created Singularity Black. Artist Stewart Semple responded by introducing the pinkest pink that everyone except Anish Kapoor can use. Can this prohibition be legally enforced? Probably not. Is it funny? Absolutely!

Welcome to the Public Domain

The Statue of Liberty is in the public domain. Venus de Milo, Mona Lisa, the Great Sphinx of Giza, the Chicago Picasso, Shakespeare's plays and sonnets, Beethoven's symphonies, works created prior to 1925 (such as Kandinsky's *Contrasting Sounds*), the U.S. Constitution, the law of gravity, the theory of relativity, teapots, geometric shapes, colors, recipes, facts, and both good and bad ideas are all in the public domain, though for a variety of different reasons.

Works that are not protected by copyright (or other intellectual property laws), for whatever reason, are referred to as being in the "public domain". As unprotected works, they are available to use without restrictions of any type. Works in the public domain can be of great value for contemporary artists in a number of ways, therefore it is advantageous to understand the broader parameters of public domain and how it applies in regard to use of available materials.

Contrasting Sounds by Wassily Kandinsky

Lavender Liberty by Mary Atwood © 2021

The public domain is the *quid pro quo* for a creator's initial monopoly. In exchange for an initial monopoly, copyrighted works "fall" into the public domain when the copyright term expires.

The public domain has been analogized to a public commons or national park. It is populated with works that either never were or are no longer eligible for copyright protection. It is a wellspring that many creative works draw on.

In this pool, there are elemental raw materials, like colors, the alphabet, descriptive facts, standard geometric forms, and other things which are categorically ineligible for copyright protection. Swimming alongside these ineligible items are earlier works of art, that due to the passage of time or other reasons, are no longer protected by copyright or other intellectual property laws.

Works that are categorically ineligible for copyright protection are in the public domain unless protected by another form of intellectual property laws such as trademark or design patent.

The Public Domain Pool by Deborah Reid © 2023

The Time Factors

Copyright does not extend to works that were created prior to the creation of copyright in 1710. All works created before the year 1710, regardless of their place of origin, are considered to be in the public domain under U.S. law, because they were created prior to the existence of any copyright law in any country.

Copyrights originally lasted for 14 years. Over the years the term increased from 14 to 28 to 56 years. In 1976, the term for works created by individuals going forward was changed to the life of the author plus 50 years. The term for works authored by corporations was increased to 75 years.

The unpublished and unregistered works of all authors who died prior to 1933 are in the public domain.

The secret diaries of Sir Arthur Conan Doyle, who died in 1930, if discovered, would be in the public domain and be free to all to use.

In 1998, the Sonny Bono Copyright Term Extension Act retroactively added 20 years to both individual and corporate terms. As a result *Steamboat Willie,* the first short featuring an early iteration of Mickey Mouse's entry into the public domain was delayed from 2004 to January 1, 2024. Later iterations of Mickey Mouse will still be protected by copyright until their terms expire. Caution: The "Mickeys" may still be protected by trademark even after copyright protection ends.

Copyright scholars have criticized the longer terms for unduly restricting the flow of material into the public domain and cutting off access by artists of all genres to a rich pool of creative material, contrary to copyright's purpose of enriching public knowledge.

Museum Collections Available

That said, the recent trend of museums making works in their collection available for use has, if not technically, practically expanded access to public domain works. Here is a small sample of the museums that now allow access to their collections:

- *Smithsonian Open Access: https://www.si.edu/openaccess*
- *V&A Collections (Victoria & Albert Museum): https://www.vam.ac.uk/collections*
- *The British Museum: https://www.britishmuseum.org/collection*
- *The Rijksmuseum Collection: https://www.rijksmuseum.nl/en/rijksstudio*
- *The Met Collection: https://www.metmuseum.org/art/collection*
- *National Gallery of Art Images: https://www.nga.gov/open-access-images.html*
- *Paris Musées (a group of 14 public museums in Paris): https://www.parismuseescollection.paris.fr/en*

In or Out of the Pool?

Figuring out what is or is not in the public domain can be complicated. There are exceptions. Additional information can be found on educational websites such as www.cornell.edu/resources/publicdomain.com.

If you are planning on using public domain works worldwide, you will need to do some research. Works in the public domain in the U.S. may still be protected by copyright in other countries with longer copyright terms.

PUBLIC ACCESS IS NOT THE SAME THING AS THE PUBLIC DOMAIN.

Just because you can download something does not mean does not mean you can legally use it.

The EXCLUSIVE RIGHTS of Copyright

Artists are given a bundle of exclusive rights in exchange for sharing their work.

THE EXCLUSIVE RIGHTS OF COPYRIGHT

Introducing the Bundle of Rights

The Current Bundle of Rights ✦ Renegotiation of the Social Bargain and the Internet Treaties
Moving Forward ✦ Divide and Conquer

Go Forth and Multiply: Reproduction Rights and Copyright

Defining Copy ✦ Some Copies in the Copyright Sense ✦ Phonorecords in the Copyright Sense
Caution: Private Copies are Copies ✦ There Are Limits

The Right to Make Derivative Works

On the Meta Level ✦ In Copyright Law ✦ A Sticky Situation ✦ Guitars + Symbols
Derivative Work v. Fair Use ✦ Limitations

Derivative Works: The Sequel

Characters Are Copyrightable

A Few Words About Fan Art and Fan Fiction

On Display, Publicly

A Short History ✦ Defining Display ✦ Some Parameters ✦ The Server Test
Other Views on Display ✦ A Cautionary Tale ✦ On Display in the Material World ✦ Limitations

The Performance Right

The Transmit Clause ✦ Private Antenna, Public Performances
One At a Time ✦ If It Quacks Like a Duck ✦ Performance Rights Organizations
Not for Profit, Not a Defense ✦ Limitations

The Distribution Right

A Long History ✦ Defining the Distribution Right ✦ It's (im)Material ✦ Public Distribution
Right of First Publication ✦ Transfers of Ownership ✦ Actually, or Not ✦ In and Out ✦ Limitations

The First Sale Doctrine

One and Done ✦ Narrow Application

Resale Royalties: Not Yet

California Dreaming

NFTs

An NFT Solution ✦ NFT and © ✦ Licenses

VARA

Droit Moral ✦ VARA Overview ✦ 5 Pointz

Introducing the Bundle of Rights

The invention of the printing press in the 15th century revolutionized the world. It facilitated the rapid reproduction of books, which had previously been handwritten. Copyright was the legal response to the exponential increase in the production of books. It is a social bargain. It provides exclusive rights as economic incentives to reward creativity and foster a dynamic culture.

The first copyright law, the Statute of Anne, provided authors and their publishers with the rights to reproduce and distribute. Subsequently, the U.S. Constitution granted Congress power to promote the "Progress of Science and the Useful Arts by securing for limited times to Authors and Inventors the exclusive Right to their respective Writings and Discoveries".

Over the years, additional rights have been formulated. Copyright law, sometimes through legislation and other times through case law, or a dialogue between the two, has continued to evolve in response to technological developments.

Bundle of Rights by Deborah Reid © 2019

The Copyright Act of 1976 is the current statutory iteration of U.S. copyright law. This Act was motivated in part by a pair of Supreme Court cases holding that cable television providers' transmission of films and shows did not infringe the copyright owners' performance rights. The Supreme Court held that as cable companies were "viewers" not "performers" their transmission was permissible. In response, Congress broadened the statutory definition of performance to specifically provide that transmission to the public is a performance of a work reserved exclusively to the copyright owners. Going forward, cable providers broadcasting without permission could be liable for copyright infringement.

The Current Bundle of Rights

The Copyright Act of 1976 grants authors the following exclusive rights:

- the right to duplicate the work (the "copy" right)
- the right to make derivative works
- the right to distribute the work
- the right to display or perform the work publicly
- the right to digitally transmit certain works
- the "making available" right

Small Bundle by Deborah Reid © 2017

Send Love by Deborah Reid © 2020

Since 1976, digital technology has revolutionized the creation, dissemination and enjoyment of copyrighted work. The Internet facilitates immediate, costless, and widespread "copying" and allows users to "send and retrieve perfect reproductions of copyrighted material easily and nearly instantaneously, to or from locations around the world across international borders."

Renegotiation of the Social Bargain and the Internet Treaties

This foundational shift caused concern among members of the World Intellectual Property Organization ("WIPO") that the international copyright regime was not keeping up with technology. WIPO is a self-funding agency of the United Nations with 193 member states, including the United States.

The information age raises issues at the heart of copyright's social bargain:

> "How can society make cultural works available to the widest possible public at affordable prices while, at the same time, assuring a dignified economic existence to creators and performers and the business associates that help them navigate the economic system? It is a question that implies a series of balances: between availability, on the one hand, and control of the distribution of works as a means of extracting value, on the other hand; between consumers and producers; between the interests of society and those of the individual creator; and between the short-term gratification of immediate consumption and the long-term process of providing economic incentives that reward creativity and foster a dynamic culture. "
>
> ~Frances Gurry, former WIPO Director, 2011

In 1996, after decades of study, the WIPO Copyright Treaty and the WIPO Performances and Phonograms Treaty (collectively, the "Internet Treaties") were completed. Because it was clear a consensus could not be reached on a single method to protect an author's right to control access to work on the Internet, a compromise "umbrella solution" was adopted.

Under the umbrella solution, treaty members are free to implement their obligations as a part of a "right of communication to the public", as a "making available right", or other rights found in their national laws.

French Umbrella by Deborah Reid © 2013

The making available right is technology neutral. It covers all formats in which a work may be digitally communicated, including downloads, streams, and any other existing or future developed methods of online transmission. The making available right focuses on access rather than receipt.

The United States has consistently maintained that its existing exclusive rights of reproduction, distribution, public performance and public display combine to provide a making available right in satisfaction of its treaty obligations. Some judges and scholars disagree.

Moving Forward

The exclusive rights included in the bundle need to be considered individually. Particular emphasis is given to the rights that have the most impact on visual art: the rights of reproduction, the right to make derivative work, and the rights of display and distribution. The performance right, the right to make phonorecords, and other examples using non-visual expression are included only to provide illustration about the interface technology and methods on particular rights.

The fundamental principles of copyright law such as originality, fixation, the elements of infringement, and fair use apply to all copyrightable work, including music. The complex statutory framework providing for mandatory and mechanical licenses for music, Performance Rights Organizations like ASCAP and BMI, are beyond the scope of this book.

Rights Triptych by Deborah Reid © 2022

Divide and Conquer

The exclusive rights are cumulative. They often overlap. For example, downloading another's image and using it on the homepage of your website implicates both the rights of reproduction and display.

The exclusive rights can be subdivided indefinitely. Each subdivision of a right may be owned and enforced separately. For example, an artist may license the use of a print of her painting as set décor for a movie and also permit the same image to reproduced on housewares and clothing. More on licensing later.

Go Forth and Multiply: Reproduction Rights and Copyright

The first right in the exclusive bundle reserved to authors is quite literally the "copy right". Authors are given the right "to reproduce the copyrighted work in Copies or Phonorecords; " This right is referred to as the duplication or reproduction right.

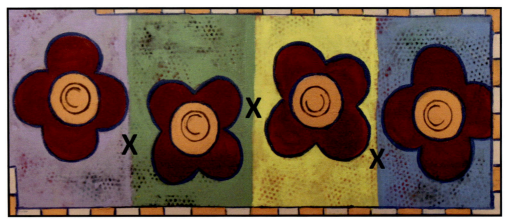

Flower Times Flower by Deborah Reid © 2022

Defining Copy

In everyday usage, copy means something that is made to look exactly like something else. The meaning in copyright law is a bit more rigorous.

A "copy" is defined as:

- a tangible form or material object in which a work is fixed by any method now known or later developed
- from which that work can be perceived, reproduced, or otherwise communicated, either directly or with the aid of a machine or device.

Some Copies in the Copyright Sense

The seminal example of the reproduction right is an author's exclusive right of multiplying copies of what he has written or printed. The right has evolved with technology. Scans of a photograph, digitization of literary works, and dubbing sound recordings from pre-existing recordings, are all copies which are reserved to the author by the reproduction right.

Artist Lee Teter regularly sold his American frontier life paintings to a gallery in Eureka Springs, Arkansas. He provided photographs of his work to post on the gallery's website to advertise his work. This arrangement continued for about a year after the gallery, its inventory, and website were sold to the Glass Onion, Inc.

When Glass Onion overhauled the gallery website, it requested and was given permission to use Teter's photographs on it. The permission was later revoked when Glass Onion refused to enter into the new Dealership Agreement proposed by Teter's management.

Glass Onion removed Teter's pictures, took their own and used those to post thumbnails and low resolution images on the website. Glass Onion maintained it was well within its rights to create and display images of the works it owned.

Teter and the Court disagreed. The Court held that the creation and storage of electronic images of Teter's copyrighted work were copies within the meaning of the Copyright Act and infringed on Teter's ownership rights.

Phonorecords in the Copyright Sense

Like copy, phonorecord is a term of art. In copyright law, phonorecords are not limited to vinyl LPs, cassette tapes, or even the segments on a hard disc, in which electronic music is encoded.

Although visual art is not reproduced in phonorecords, the landmark phonorecord case, *Capital Records v ReDigi* provides important guidance on how technology interfaces with the reproduction right.

In 2009, John Ossenmacher and Larry Rudolph, a former Principal Research Scientist at MIT, founded ReDigi to create enabling technology for the lawful resale of digital music files initially purchased from Apple iTunes and similar services. ReDigi went to great lengths to design a process that would not violate a copyright owner's right of reproduction.

The first step in the process was for an iTunes purchaser to download and install ReDigi's Music Manager software program onto their personal device. ReDigi's software then

Victrola by Mary Atwood © 2023

broke the music file into small data blocks which were copied, transmitted, and deleted sequentially. This differed from conventional methods of data migration because the entire file never existed in two places simultaneously.

The record companies who had licensed their sound recordings to Apple iTunes were not persuaded and sued for copyright infringement. The 2nd Circuit rejected ReDigi's categorization of the process as a transfer rather than a reproduction. In the course of transferring a digital music file from the original purchaser's computer to a new purchaser, the receipt and storage on ReDigi's server and again on the new purchaser's device created digital files in new material objects of more than transitory duration properly, which created new phonorecords and violated the reproduction right.

Caution: Private Copies are Copies

Making unauthorized copies and phonorecords is a violation of the reproduction right. Copies of webpages stored automatically in a computer's cache or RAM for more than a fleeting moment fall within the Copyright Act's definition of copies.

This is true whether or not the copy is sold. Automatic cache pages created by non-commercial users are protected by the fair use doctrine.

CAVEAT CREATOR ♦ ARTIST BEWARE

There are Limits

There are limitations on the scope of the reproduction right and the other exclusive rights. The First Sale Doctrine and the Fair Use Doctrine are important limitations with long histories, wide application and substantial impact on each of the exclusive rights. These doctrines are discussed in following sections.

There are also numerous narrow statutory limitations on the exclusive rights which allow for use of copyrighted material without permission. For example, libraries are permitted to make one copy of a work if it is not used commercially, directly or indirectly, without permission of the copyright owner.

A chart of the statutory limitations for each exclusive right is included at the end of the discussion for that right.

Limitations on the Reproduction Right

Copyright Act Provisions	Exemptions
108	Reproduction by libraries and archives
112	Ephemeral recordings
113 (c)	Pictures and photographs of useful articles
114	Sound recordings
115	Mechanical compulsory licenses for non-dramatic musical works
117	Computer program by owner necessary to utilize or maintain program
121, 121A	Literary works for the blind and disabled

The Right to Make Derivative Works

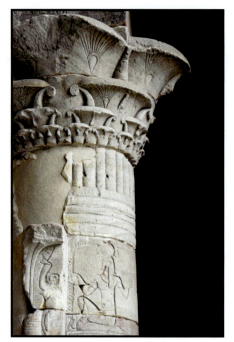

Timeless by Mary Atwood © 2021

"The thing that hath been, it is that which shall be; and that which is done is that which shall be done: and there is no new thing under the sun."

Ecclesiastes 1:9

On the Meta Level

In the grand scheme of things, everything is derivative. Every book in literature, science, and art borrows, and must necessarily borrow and use, much of which was well known and used before.

In Copyright Law

The term derivative is not as far reaching in copyright law usage. It is also not pejorative, as in "Oh, his work is so derivative." In copyright law, derivative works are by definition based on one or more preexisting works. The right to make derivative works is one of the rights in the author's exclusive bundle. It is often referred to as the adaptation right.

The right to make derivative works is reserved to the copyright owner. The copyright owner has the right to prepare or authorize someone else to create a derivative work. This right may be transferred in whole or in part. For example, the author of a best-selling novel may authorize a playwright to write a play based on the novel and license someone else to write a screenplay.

A change in the medium, rather than the message or content, is often an indication of a derivative work.

Here are some examples in the visual arts:

- Drawing ---------Sculpture ------------ (and back again)
- Photograph ----------- Painting
- Painting -------------- Lithograph

Unauthorized derivative works are copyright infringements. It is a violation of the author's exclusive right to make derivative works without permission.

A Sticky Situation

Antioch Company was the copyright owner of sheets of pictorial stickers and idea books of sticker combinations. Its competitor, Scrapbook Borders, used Antioch's campsite sticker series and a few other Antioch stickers as a decorative scrap book page in its own idea book.

Read Happy Tapir by Deborah Reid © 2023

Antioch did not like the idea and sued. Scrapbook Borders argued its unauthorized use showcased the artistic potential of the stickers and promoted Antioch's sales. Scrapbook Borders' argument was soundly and roundly rejected. Scrapbook Border's use of the stickers was an unauthorized derivative work that infringed on Antioch's copyright.

Although regularly voiced in and outside of the courtroom, "They should be flattered" or "I am giving them valuable exposure" is not a defense to copyright infringement. Although adapting someone else's work may be intended as a homage, it is also an infringement of the exclusive right to make derivative works reserved to the copyright owner.

Guitars + Symbols

The artist formerly known as Prince referred to himself by use of a symbol registered with the U.S. Copyright Office as a work of visual art beginning in 1992. Authorized licensees used the symbol in jewelry, clothing, and musical instruments.

Pickett made a guitar embodying the symbol, which he claimed to have shown to Prince. Shortly afterwards, Prince played a strikingly similar guitar in public and was boldly sued by Pickett for copyright infringement. In essence, Pickett claimed that Prince's embodiment of Prince's copyrighted symbol in a guitar was an infringement of Pickett's prior unauthorized embodiment of Prince's copyrighted symbol in a guitar.

Not surprisingly, Pickett lost. Pickett's recasting of a two-dimensional drawing into a three dimensional object is a classic derivative work. The right to make such a derivative work belonged to the copyright owner, Prince. Prince's recasting of his symbol into a guitar was an exercise of his exclusive right to make or authorize derivative works.

Derivative Work v. Fair Use

Defendants in infringement lawsuits often argue that their use of someone else's work is a "fair use". Defendants often lose.

Shades of Gray with Butterfly by Mary Atwood and Deborah Reid © 2021

Fair use is the right to use copyrighted material without permission or payment in some circumstances. It is based on the recognition that some copyrighted materials are valuable to society. It is a defense to copyright infringement.

The distinction between a derivative use exclusive to the author and a permissible fair use by others is not often black and white. They are both about change. A derivative work may express the same idea in the same or a different medium. A fair use often comments on the original or conveys a different message.

Limitations on the Right to Make Derivative Works

Copyright Act Provisions	Exemptions
114 (b)	Sound recordings
115(a) (2)	Non-dramatic musical works
120	Architectural works

Derivative Works: The Sequel

Sequels are derivative works. They are adaptations. The right to make sequels of contemporary novels such as Harry Potter and the Philosopher's Stone, superhero movies like Batman, and video games like Duke Nukem, belongs to the copyright owner.

Sequels by Mary Atwood © 2022

The rights to Duke Nukem 3D, a popular computer game played from the perspective of its title character, a beefy commando type who wanders around post-apocalyptic Los Angeles lobbing hand grenades and avoiding radioactive slime in order to advance to the next level, were owned by FormGen ,Inc. The game included a Build Editor for players to create their own levels, which they can post on the Internet for others to download. Micro Star, a computer software distributor, did just that: It downloaded 300 user-created levels and stamped them onto a CD, which it then sold commercially as Nuke It (N/I). While the Duke Nukem players had permission to create their own levels, the permission did not extend to Micro Star.

When sued, Micro Star argued there was no infringement, as its CD only included instructions to access the FormGen's art source library rather than the actual copyrighted images from the Duke Nukem art source library.

The 9th Circuit explained that the Micro Star CD was a derivative work that infringed, even though no actual copying of FormGen's images occurred. The stories told in the "NI/MAP files were surely sequels telling new (though somewhat repetitive) tales of Duke's fabulous adventures. A book about Duke Nukem would infringe for the same reason, even if it contained no pictures."

Characters are Copyrightable

Cartoons and comic strips are types of work eligible for copyright protection. Drawings, picture depictions and written descriptions of a character can be registered for copyright.

A Few Words About Fan Art and Fan Fiction

Copyright Infringement. Really. Mostly.

Fan art is a drawing based on a character, costume, or location that is made without permission by the original creator. Fan fiction uses established characters, settings and other intellectual property to continue or tell a new story. The vast majority of Fan Art and Fan Fiction are derivative works which, if not authorized by the copyright owner, are copyright infringements. Fan art and fan fiction are sequels.

Again, "they should be flattered" is not a defense to copyright infringement. The copyright owners of popular and profitable cartoon and other characters place a high value on their copyrights and often use DMCA take down notices for online infringements. Although usually financially untenable, lawsuits for injunctions and damages are also possible.

CX2 by Deborah Reid © 2023

For example, when Axanar Productions produced and made an unauthorized twenty-one minute film *Star Trek: Prelude to Axanar* available for free online to raise money for an intended full length film which was intended to be an "authentic and independent film true to the Star Trek canon". Paramount Pictures filed suit in short order

The matter was settled by the parties shortly after the United States District Court for the Central District of California ruled that Axanar's film was a derivative work and not a fair use of copyrighted work by Axanar. As part of the settlement, Axanar agreed to adhere to Paramount's fan-film guidelines in the future.

In very few instances, work using a character or other intellectual property in a way that meets the requirements of the fair use is permissible.

On Display, Publicly

A Short History

The display right is the most recent addition to the copyright owner's exclusive bundle of rights. Its 1976 introduction was intended to fill in the gaps where advancing technology could transmit or display a work without the creation of an actual copy that would violate the right of reproduction.

A Moment by Deborah Reid © 2023

When the display right was conceived the words "tweet", "viral", and "embed" invoked thoughts of a bird, a disease, and a reporter. These terms have new meanings online, where images are shared with dizzying speed. The changes in vocabulary and technology mean that the operation of the display right is a "work in progress" at this time.

Initially, the expansive definition of copy formulated by courts to determine the scope of the reproduction right occupied much of the territory the display right was intended to fill. That has started to change.

Defining Display

The exclusive right to publicly display a work is reserved to the artist in particular instances. The definition of display, in the copyright context, means:

- Showing a work or its copy
- Publicly
- In person or by transmission
- By processes or methods now known or later developed

Some Parameters

The display right applies to the visual arts, literary, musical, dramatic, and choreographic works, and individual images in audiovisual works and motion pictures. Displaying a movie is different from "performing" a movie. Showing an audiovisual work in sequence is protected by the performance right. Showing individual images from an audiovisual work is restricted by the display right. The display right also does not extend to sound recordings and architectural works.

Only unauthorized displays made publicly infringe the display right. Many important everyday displays are exempt from its coverage. For example, teacher and student displays during face-to-face teaching are perfectly permissible. So are displays made in the course of a religious service. The full range of statutory exemptions are listed in the limitation chart at the end of this section.

Here are some examples of how the display right plays out, both on and offline.

The Server Test

The online unauthorized showing of nude photographs gave rise to the server test.

Perfect 10 marketed and sold copyrighted images of nude models online. It claimed that both thumbnails and "framed" full size images generated in response to Google image searches were infringements of its display right.

Perfect 10 scored 50 percent. In 2007, the 9th Circuit formulated the server test, which determines liability for infringement by the server where the image is stored or hosted. The thumbnail images which appeared automatically were stored on Google's server, and therefore infringed the display right. The full size images that appeared in response to clicking on the thumbnail were not on Google's server. These images were communicated directly from another's webpage in response to the HTML instructions supplied by Google. Therefore, there was no copyright infringement by Google with regard to the full size images.

Send Love Triptych by Deborah Reid © 2022

Ultimately, both of Google's practices were found to be a protected fair use that did not infringe on Perfect 10's copyrights.

Other Views on Display

Not all courts who have looked at the display right in an online context have agreed with the 9th Circuit's server test.

Justin Goldman's copyrighted photo of football legend Tom Brady went viral on social media. Breitbart News and other online news outlets featured Goldman's photograph on their websites by embedding it into articles about whether Tom Brady would help seal a deal between the Boston Celtics and basketball player Kevin Durant.

In response to Goldman's infringement suit, the news outlets argued that their use passed the server test. They contend it was permissible because the photo had not been hosted on their servers. The webpages viewed by their readers were seamless mixes of text and images. The image was "embedded" by use of codes, provided by social media sites, to HTML instructions incorporating an image on a third-party server.

Judge Katherine B. Forrest, of the influential Southern District of New York bench, found that Goldman's display right had been infringed. She found that the legislative history and subsequent Supreme Court cases provided no basis for a rule that the physical location or possession should determine whether an infringement occurred. The mechanics of how the images were shown are overshadowed by the fact that the defendants visibly showed - displayed - the image without permission.

A Cautionary Tale

Yes, but Be Careful by Mary Atwood © 2022

When Stephanie Sinclair, another professional photographer, brought suit against Mashable for displaying her photograph on its website without her permission, she lost. Ms. Sinclair had posted her photograph on her Instagram public account. Pursuant to the Instagram terms and conditions in force at the time, images that were posted on public accounts were subject to Instagram's Application Programming Interface. The terms in effect at the time allowed others to embed publicly-posted content in their own websites.

Judge Kimba Wood acknowledged that the choice to forego posting on one of the most popular public photo sharing platforms or agreeing to the Application Programming Interface ("API") presented a dilemma to Sinclair, a professional photographer. However, by posting to a public account, Sinclair chose to agree to the terms of the API. The court could not release Sinclair from the agreement she made.

Instagram revised its terms. It does not grant sublicenses. The platform's policies now require users to obtain licenses where necessary from the rights holder. This could change again. You need to check.

Moral of the Story: Read the Terms and Conditions and Terms of Agreement of platforms you sign up for. When you hit "click", it's a contract.

On Display in the Material World

The protection of the display right is not limited to images on computer screens. However, when it comes to displays in the material world, the exceptions seem to cover more ground than the rule.

Creative Expression by Deborah Reid © 2023

Most commonplace real world displays are covered by a big common-sense exception: Owners of actual artworks or lawfully made copies (the "owned work") have the right to publicly display it to viewers where the owned work is located.

This exception is based on the logical premise that people should be able to display copyrighted work they own without seeking permission from the author. If not, anyone wearing clothing made from a copyrighted fabric design would need permission to walk down the street. This exception enables collectors to loan work to museums and galleries to exhibit works for sale without the need for releases.

Oddly, this exception also extends to the projection of an image of the work to viewers who are present at the same place where the work is located. For example, a museum displaying XYZ as a part of the 123 show could project an image of XYZ to illustrate a lecture at the museum. The museum could not include it in a slide show given off museum premises.

A case that has been described as "the ultimate how-not-to guide in the complicated world of installation art" provides insight on how the display right operates in the material world of visual art. Artist Christoph Buchel's football-field-sized art installation "Training Ground for Democracy" was to be exhibited at MASS MoCA.

The problems started when Buchel and MASS MoCA failed to put their agreement regarding their relationship or intellectual property rights into writing. Things went downhill from there. The installation was started but not completed.

Litigation commenced. MASS MoCA asked the court for an order stating that it had the right to show the work. Buchel asked the court for an order preventing MASS MoCA from showing the unfinished installation to the public.

The court stated that MASS MoCA's repeated and deliberate exhibition of the unfinished installation to numerous individuals would violate the display right. Because the ownership of the work was murky, further proceedings were ordered for a determination of whether MASS MoCA was entitled as owner of the installation to display it.

Moral of the Story: Write agreements down. It brings important issues into focus and manages expectations.

Limitations on the Display Right

Copyright Act Provision	Exemptions
110(a)	Face-to-face teaching activities in classroom or similar place
110(2)	Instructional transmissions
110(3)	Religious services
113(c)	Pictures or photographs of useful articles
111(a), 111 (c) (1) 110 (5)	Certain secondary transmissions
118 (c) (1) 37 CFR 253.8	Compulsory license for noncommercial broadcasting

The Performance Right

The display right and the performance right are similar in structure but are applicable to different forms of creative expression. Like the display right, the performance right is exclusive to the author in public. You can sing whatever you want in your shower.

Unlike the display right, the performance right does not apply to pictorial, sculptural or graphic works. You cannot perform a painting, a sculpture, or a poster.

The performance right applies to literary, dramatic, musical, choreographic, pantomime, and other audiovisual works. A play can be performed, as can songs, poems, and movies.

The interplay between judicial interpretation and legislation of the performance right is a prime example of how the U.S. copyright law is evolving in response to technology.

The Careless Dancer by Mary Atwood © 2010

The Transmit Clause

The Transmit Clause in the Copyright Act of 1976 was added by Congress to correct earlier Supreme Court rulings that unlicensed cable television transmissions of movies and television programs did not infringe performance rights.

The Transmit Clause provides that the performance right includes the right to:

> "transmit or otherwise communicate a performance of the work to the public, by means of any device or process, whether the members of the public receive it in the same or in separate places at the same or different times."

Private Antenna, Public Performances

Aereo, Inc. used a system designed to skirt the scope of the public performance right to stream copyrighted material over the Internet. Aereo housed thousands of dime-sized antennas, along with transcoders and servers, in a centralized warehouse. Aereo subscribers selected shows from a menu on its website. An antenna assigned to the subscriber tuned to a broadcast carrying the selected show. The signals received were translated into Internet transmittable data, saved in subscriber specific folders, and streamed to the subscriber after several seconds of programming was saved.

ABC, Inc., and other copyright owners sued for infringement of their exclusive right of performance. Aereo took the position that it was merely an equipment provider. Aereo's arguments that its services were not a public performance were successful at the trial and appellate levels. Things changed at the Supreme Court.

One at a Time

The Transmit Clause applies to multiple transmissions of the same work. The transmissions do not have to be simultaneous. You transmit a message to your friends, whether you send a single email to many or several separate emails to each friend, or post the same message on Facebook.

Aereo's argument that because personal antennas transmitted subscriber-specific copies, it was not transmitting "to the public" was also unsuccessful. Aereo transmitted the broadcasts to large numbers of people who were unrelated and unknown to each other - "the public".

If it Quacks Like a Duck. . . .

Peking Duck by Mary Atwood © 2009

Aereo maintained that it was different from the earlier cable systems targeted by the Transmit Clause because its system remained inert until a subscriber selected a program. In simpler terms, it did not transmit constantly. Despite this technological difference, the Supreme Court held that an entity that acts like a cable tv system "performs" even if it is simply enhancing a subscriber's ability to receive broadcast signals. Aereo's tiny antennas and personalized transmissions did not skirt the enhanced performance right. It infringed on the copyright owners' exclusive right of performance.

Performance Rights Organizations

The fundamental principles of copyright law apply to all copyrightable works. A complex statutory framework that deals only with music is built on this foundation. This framework provides for mandatory and mechanical licenses, and performance rights organizations like ASCAP and BMI.

This area is beyond the scope of this tome. For further guidance check out *The Musicians' Guide to Music Copyright Law* by Jim Jesse.

Not for Profit, Not a Defense

"But it's for charity," is an often-used excuse for copyright infringement in cases where no profit is involved. However, a public performance of someone else's copyrighted work, for charity or other noble purpose, is still a public performance of someone else's work. It is a copyright infringement.

That said, some charitable, educational, or religious performances have been given a statutory exemption from the exclusive rights and are not copyright infringements.

Limitations on the Performance Right

Copyright Act Provisions	Exemptions
110 (1)	Face to face teaching activities
110 (2)	Instructional transmissions
110(3)	Religious services
110(4)	Nonprofit performances not by transmission without direct or indirect fees
110 (6)	Annual agricultural or horticultural fairs or exhibits
110 (7)	Vending establishments
110 (8), (9)	Transmissions to handicapped persons
110 (10)	Fraternal organizations
110 (11)	Making limited portions of audio or video content of motion pictures imperceptible
118	Compulsory license for noncommercial broadcasting
116	Compulsory license for jukeboxes
111, 119, 122	Compulsory license for certain secondary transmissions

The Distribution Right

A Long History

Historically, the dissemination of works and their copies have dominated the economy of copyright. The distribution right is an important tool for copyright owners to monetize their work. Like the reproduction right, it has existed since the inception of copyright. Its terminology and parameters have evolved over the years in response to changes in markets and technology.

Previously, U.S. copyright law provided copyright owners with the rights to "publish" and "vend". Over the years, the terms "publish" and "publication" acquired a lot of baggage. There were many interpretations, some of which were conflicting. The jurisprudence was dense and confusing. New terminology was adopted to clear things up.

Since 1976, copyright owners have had "the exclusive right to distribute copies of the work to the public by sale, or by rental or lease or lending." This statutory iteration of the right was drafted when most distributions involved hard copies and physical transfers. Things have changed.

There are some holes in its coverage. There are big questions about whether the distribution right does, can or should provide a "making available" right. Holes and all, the distribution right remains an economically important right for artists.

Defining the Distribution Right

A copyright owner has the exclusive right to distribute copies or phonorecords of the work, publicly, to authorize the same and prevent distribution of infringing copies. This right is closely aligned with the rights of importation and exportation.

The defining elements of the distribution right are:

- copies and phonorecords
- public
- distribution by sale or by rental or lease or lending

As you may have surmised, these terms all have a particularized meaning in the copyright context. Particularly, "copies and phonorecords".

It's (im)Material

How phonorecords play out in the distribution right illustrates how copies are defined.

In *London Sire v. Does 1,* several large record companies sued individual computer users using "peer to peer" file-sharing software to download and disseminate copyrighted music without paying for it. The file-sharers argued that purely electronic file-sharing could not possibly infringe the distribution right which covered only "copies and phonorecords of the copyrighted work" both defined in the Copyright Act as "material objects".

In rejecting this argument, the Court explained that materiality as used in the Copyright Act does not mean the same thing as it does in ordinary usage. Its scope is not limited to tangible physical objects like books or vinyl records. Materiality is a term of art referencing a medium in which a copyrighted work can be fixed. A work is fixed in a tangible medium when its embodiment in a copy or a phonorecord is sufficiently permanent or stable to allow it to be perceived, reproduced, or otherwise communicated for more than a transitory period.

Any media in which a sound recording can be fixed, including electronic files, is a "material object" in copyright law. When a user on a peer-to-peer network downloads a song from another user, she receives a digital sequence which is magnetically encoded on her hard disk or written on other media.

Public Distribution

Only distribution to the public implicates the distribution right. If you print a bunch of unauthorized copies of a copyrighted photograph and keep them in your desk drawer you have not infringed the distribution right. You can even give a few copies to family and friends without infringing the distribution right. However, in either instance, you will have infringed the reproduction right.

Right of First Publication

In addition to giving the copyright owner some control over the disposition of the physical objects, the distribution right includes a right of first publication or disclosure. The copyright owner is entitled to authorize or prohibit the first sale of the copy of the work.

Shortly after leaving the White House, former President Gerald R. Ford contracted with Harper & Row and Readers Digest to publish his unwritten memoirs and the exclusive right to prepublication excerpts. Harper & Row, in turn, granted Time magazine the exclusive right to excerpt 7500 words of the memoir about the Nixon pardon.

A few weeks prior to Time's planned publication, a clandestine copy of the manuscript was given to the editor of another magazine, *The Nation*. A 2250-word article composed of verbatim quotes, paraphrases, and facts drawn exclusively from the manuscript was hurriedly assembled and published by *The Nation*.

The Supreme Court ruled *The Nation* violated Ford's right of first public distribution, which implicated both his personal interest in creative control and valuable property interest in prepublication rights. It also rejected *The Nation*'s assertion of First Amendment protections and fair use.

Transfers of Ownership

The exclusive right applies only to distribution "by sale, rental, lease or lending". The equation of distribution to a transfer of ownership or possession was contemplated in an analog environment. When a bookstore sells a book it has one less copy in its inventory. Typically, when a digital file is transferred the sender retains the original in its computer memory. The courts have found distribution occurs when a new copy to be owned by the recipient is created.

Actually, or Not

The courts and commentators consistently agree that when a public library makes a work in its collection available to the public for browsing or borrowing, it has distributed the work. A distribution has occurred. Proof of actual browsing or borrowing is not required.

This consistency deteriorates in the digital domain. U.S. Courts, commentators and the U.S. Copyright Office all agree that providing digital access to copyrighted works without authorization *may* infringe the distribution right. Maybe not.

Napster started providing its pioneering music peer-to-peer file sharing services online in 1999. Napster's integrated system allowed users to: (1) make MP3 music files stored on individual computer hard drives available for copying by other Napster users; (2) search for MP3 music files stored on other users' computers; and (3) transfer and download exact copies of the contents of other users' MP3 files from one computer to another via the Internet. This system clearly violated the distribution right of the record companies who owned the copyrights on the majority of music being shared on Napster's peer-to-peer network.

The Long Room by Deborah Reid © 2022

What Courts don't agree on is whether or not a transfer must actually be completed for a distribution to occur. Some courts have held that an online offer to make copyrighted material available is itself a distribution. Other courts have held that evidence of an actual download is required to prove that a distribution has occurred. This inconsistency raised the issue of whether the distribution right and other exclusive rights in the bundle actually provide a "making available" right.

In and Out

Importation into the United States and exportation from the United States without permission of the copyright owner can infringe the distribution right.

The distribution right, including the rights to limit importation and exportation, is limited by the First Sale Doctrine.

Money Makes the World Go Round by Mary Atwood © 2018

Limitations on the Distribution Right

Copyright Act Provisions	Exemptions
108	Library distribution
115, 118	Nondramatic musical works
114(b)	Sound recordings
113(c)	Pictures and photographs of useful articles
121 + 121A	Literary works for the blind and disabled

The First Sale Doctrine

One and Done

The first sale doctrine provides a defense to infringement of the distribution right. A copyright owner's right to control distribution is limited to the initial distribution – aka the first sale – of the work.

Once the copyright owner puts a work into the stream of commerce the distribution right is exhausted.

After the title to a work is transferred by a sale or similar transaction, the purchaser is free to resell the work, display it publicly.

Libraries, used book and record stores, and even garage sales are all made possible by the first sale doctrine. Your ability to walk down the street wearing a garment made out of a copyrighted fabric without permission of the fabric designer is also because of the first sale doctrine.

Bargain Books by Mary Atwood © 2023

Narrow Application

The first sale doctrine is very narrow. It applies only to the actual, physical work sold. No rights are granted as to the underlying work. Purchasers of books, sculptures, and/or photographs do not have the right to reproduce or adapt the work. They cannot print an image of the work on a T-shirt or anything else absent permission of the copyright owner. The copyright does not transfer with the physical work. The copyright remains with the author or other copyright owner unless agreed to otherwise.

The first sale doctrine has not been extended to digital sales. For example, in *ReDigi* the first sale doctrine did not provide a defense for a digital platform that allowed users to purchase and sell songs that had been lawfully purchased from Apple's iTunes stores. The process, which involved at least one unauthorized copy, violated the reproduction right.

The first sale doctrine does, however, extend to copies lawfully manufactured overseas. Those copies may be legally imported into the United States.

Resale Royalties: Not Yet

An artist resale royalty, or *"droit de suite"*, provides artists with an opportunity to benefit from the increased value of their works over time by granting them a percentage of the proceeds from the resale of their original works of art. The resale royalty originated in France in the 1920s. It is part of the copyright law of more than 70 countries, including most of Europe.

Sotheby's by Deborah Reid © 2019

Resale royalties are not currently included in the exclusive rights afforded to copyright owners under the U.S. law. The first sale doctrine permits the lawful owner of a copyrighted work "to sell or otherwise dispose of the possession of that copy" and to "display that copy publicly . . ." without the authorization of the creator.

Consequently, in most instances, only the initial sale of a work of visual art inures to the benefit of the artist. Collectors and other purchasers reap any increase in that work's value over time.

California Dreaming

In 1977, California enacted the California Resale Royalty Act ("CRAA") granting artists an unwaivable 5% royalty on resales to address the inequity.

In 2011, Chuck Close and Laddie John Dill brought a class action suit in California against Sotheby's, Christie's, and eBay to recover unpaid royalties. They lost. The 9th Circuit struck down the California statute on the grounds that it impermissibly reshaped the contours of the first sale doctrine and was preempted by federal copyright law.

Acts which extend the resale rights to artists have been introduced to Congress on several occasions but have yet to become law.

NFTs

An NFT Solution?

NFTs typically provide for resale royalties contractually as part of the NFT. This has made them an inviting avenue for artists.

NFT stands for "non-fungible token". Fungible means interchangeable. For examples, one dollar bill is worth the same as another dollar bill. NFTs each contain unique identifying data which is NON fungible.

The tokens are blockchain based tokens stored in digital wallets. When you purchase an NFT you get a digital Certificate of Ownership registered on the block chain, a digital distributed ledger system. Blockchain is harder to hack because the data is not located in a central depository. It is like an email with "reply to all" being the only option.

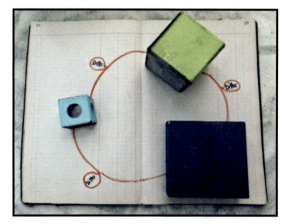

Blockchain Ledger by Deborah Reid © 2021

NFT and ©

Any piece of digital media can be attached to an NFT. Copyright's scope protection for writings encompasses pictorial, graphic art, sculptures and computer code. It includes the art and music loaded onto the token and most probably any code used to do so.

NFT can be issued as single editions like an original painting or in a series like a limited edition print. Unlike a print or a painting, no physical art is involved.

The default rule is that when a piece of art is sold the copyright remains with the artist who retains the exclusive rights to reproduce, make derivative works, display or perform the work applies to NFTs.

Absent contractual provisions to the contrary, an NFT purchaser obtains only a digital certificate of ownership. A purchaser does not get any physical art or the right to reproduce the digital media on the NFT. The exclusive rights are not transferred.

Licenses

Licenses, like provisions for resale royalties, are sometimes included in NFTs. For example, Cryptokitties allowed for commercial uses for up $100,000.00 per year. The license for *NBA Top Shots* prohibited the use of purchased NFTs for marketing and sale of products or services.

If you are going to mint an NFT make sure that you own the copyright or have a license to reproduce the contents. An NFT with a digital image of Basquiat's *Pagoda With Comb* was pulled from auction when the Basquiat estate objected to the unlicensed illicit reproduction.

VARA

Droit Moral

"*Droit moral*" is a French term for "moral rights". It refers to the personal rights creators have in their work. It protects artistic integrity and prevents others from altering the work of artists, or removing the artist's name from work without the artist's permission.

Our Lady of Paris by Mary Atwood © 2018

Droit moral is a recognition that the process of creating requires an investment of personality and deserves protection on its own. These rights emanate from the act of authorship itself. Unlike copyright, it is not meant to be economically driven.

Droit moral originated in France. It has been accepted and adopted by every civil law system in the European Union. It is recognized in the civil law countries of Latin America, Africa and Asia. India and Israel have enacted moral rights legislation.

VARA Overview

Droit moral has limited application in the United States through the Visual Artist Rights Act of 1990 (VARA). VARA provides limited rights of attribution and integrity to some visual artists for some works.

VARA protections are only available for works of fine art such as paintings or sculptures. Prints and photographs in editions of 200 or less, signed by the artist, may also qualify for VARA protection.

No work is protected unless it is of "recognized stature". No work for hire is eligible for VARA protection. VARA rights die with the artist.

If a mural or sculpture attached to a structure is a qualifying work, the artist must be given 90 days to remove the work before it can be modified or destroyed. This right, and other VARA rights, are waivable by contract.

5 Pointz

5 Pointz in Long Island City, NY was the repository of the largest collection of exterior aerosol art in the United States. In response to its planned demolition, 21 aerosol artists filed suit seeking a preliminary injunction under the Visual Artists Rights Act of 1990 ("VARA") to prevent the destruction of their works on the warehouse buildings.

Phoenix Art District, Jacksonville, FL by Mary Atwood © 2023

The artists presented expert testimony regarding the stature of the artists and value of the work. After the trial judge refused to issue an injunction preventing the demolition of the buildings at a later date, the property owner had the work whitewashed in the middle of the night without giving the required 90 day notice to the artists. None of the works were salvageable.

The trial judge found that forty-three of the works qualified for VARA protection and awarded the artists close to seven million dollars in statutory damages.

The 2nd Circuit affirmed. It held that the potentially temporary nature of street art does not keep it from being works of a recognized stature. The court referenced Christo's temporary works and Banksy's street art as works of significant artistic merit and cultural importance as examples.

The OWNERSHIP of Copyright

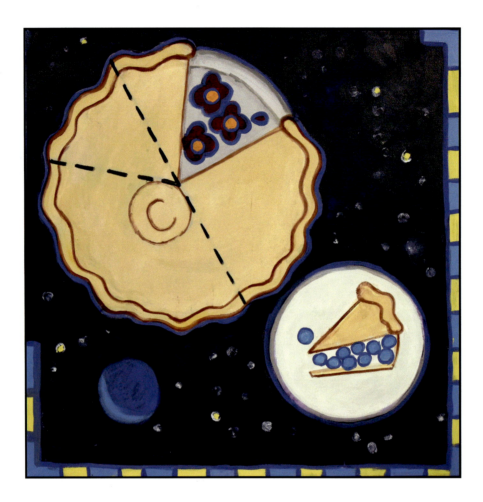

Artists automatically own the copyright in their original works upon creation.
The copyright can be divided and subdivided. Works made for hire are different.

THE OWNERSHIP OF COPYRIGHT

An Overview of Ownership

Who Can Be an Author

Authors or Proprietors ♦ Learned Men and Pseudonymous Women ♦ Citizenship
Animals Need Not Apply ♦ Deus ex Machina ♦ People Not Machines ♦ Artificial Intelligence is (Not)
BIG Questions and Copyright Issues ♦ The Output ♦ Zarya of the Dawn and The U.S. Copyright Answer
How Much is Enough? ♦ Some OBVIOUSly Different Answers
Input: What Feeds AI? Does it Infringe Copyrights?
License to Train ♦ Q: Fair Use? A: It Depends ♦ Moving Forward

Collaborations, Co-Authors, Commissions, and Compilations

The Statutory Framework ♦ Defining Lines ♦ Intent: To Be, or Not to Be, a Co-Author
Nature of the Contribution: Copyrightable, or Not ♦ A Comic Book Case Study
Co-Ownership of the Count ♦ Medieval Spawn ♦ The Consequences of Co-Authorship
Royalties Are Different

Works Made for Hire

What Are Works Made for Hire? ♦ Works Created by Employees in the Scope of Employment
The Second Situation ♦ There Are Consequences ♦ 7 Questions

Assignments and Transfers

Introduction ♦ What is an Assignment?

Licenses

Why Use a License? ♦ License This, License That ♦ How to Create a License ♦ By Implication
CopyLEFT ♦ Creative Commons ♦ 3 Things, 4 Components, and 6+ Licenses ♦ It is Forever, for Some

An Overview of Ownership

We first surveyed the types of work eligible for copyright protection, as well as the threshold requirements of originality and fixation for copyrightability. Next, we examined the bundle of exclusive rights conferred on authors. Now, we will explain the ownership of copyright.

We will open with authorship. In copyright parlance, the person who fixes an original work in a tangible medium of expression is referred to as an author. This holds true whether the work is a book, sculpture, painting, cartoon, architectural plan or other type of work eligible for copyright protection. Who can and cannot be an author will be discussed.

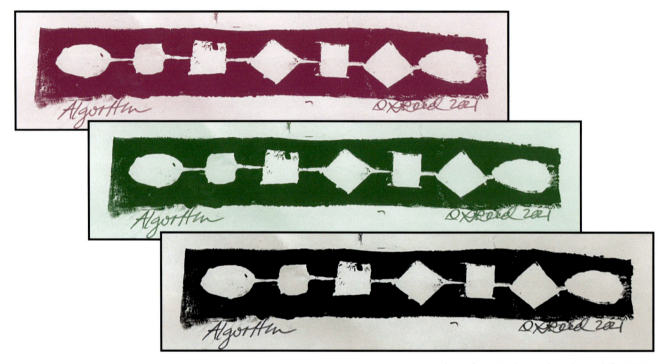

Algorithm Trio by Deborah Reid © 2023

As a general rule, copyright ownership belongs to the author upon creation. Like most rules, there are exceptions. The impact of collaboration, co-authorship and commissions will be explored. The specific requirements of works made for hire, and the major exception to the rule, will also be detailed.

Methods for transferring ownership of copyright, in whole or in part, will then be reviewed. We will wrap up with a summary of current licensing schemes and alternative regimes available to artists.

Who Can Be an Author

Authors or Proprietors

The very first copyright statute, the Statute of Anne, begins with the following preamble:

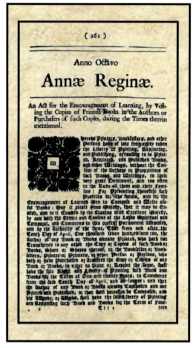

Statute of Anne

> "Whereas printers, Booksellers, and other Persons have of late frequently taken the liberty of Printing, Reprinting and Publishing, or causing to be Printed, Reprinted, and Published Books and other Writings, without the consent of the Authors or Proprietors of such Books and Writings, to their very great Detriment, and too often to the Ruin of them and their Families: For Preventing therefore such Practices for the future, and for the Encouragement of Learned men to Compose and Write useful Books. . . . ."

The U.S. Constitution gives Congress the power:

> "To promote the Progress of Science and the useful Arts by securing for limited times to Authors and Inventors the exclusive Right to their respective Writings and Discoveries."

As the subject matter of copyright expanded beyond writings to include sculpture, photographs, movies, screenplays and architecture, the word "author" came to include practitioners of those disciplines.

This use of author continues in the current U.S. copyright statutes, which provide for ownership of the right to vest initially in the author or authors of the work. Author is used to refer to the person responsible for the creation of any copyrightable work.

Learned Men and Pseudonymous Women

Copyright itself was created "for the encouragement of Learned Men". Over the years, learned women have been discouraged. Although there has never been a requirement for authors to be male, there is a long history of women using male or gender-neutral names to avoid discrimination, condescension and dismissal of their work.

Pseudonymous Women by Mary Atwood © 2022

Mary Ann Evans famously used the pen name George Eliot for *Middlemarch, Silas Marner* and *The Mill on the Floss*. Before *Little Women*, Louisa May Alcott wrote as A.M. Barnard. Emily, Charlotte, and Anne Bronte sometimes wrote as Ellis, Currer, and Acton Bell, respectively. Joanne Rowling used J.K. Rowling so the Harry Potter books would be more appealing to boys.

June Tarpé Mills was a pioneering cartoonist and the creator of Miss Fury, the first female comic book superhero (*or heroine*) to be created by a female. She signed her works as Tarpé Mills. Elaine de Koonig signed her abstract expressionist masterpieces with initials only.

Pseudonyms continue to be used in response to sexism and for many other reasons. Copyright law includes specific rules for pseudonyms. A work registered under a pseudonym lasts for the 95 years from the date of publication or 120 years from the date of creation, whichever is shorter. Its duration is likely to be shorter. Other copyrights span the life of the author plus 70 years.

Citizenship

- You do not need to be a U.S. citizen to register a copyright with the U.S. Copyright Office.
- All unpublished copyrightable works are eligible for U.S. copyright registration.
- Published works must have "points of attachment" to the United States for registration.

Some examples of points of attachment are the U.S. residency or citizenship of the author at the time of first publication. Initial publication in the U.S., or other country party to certain intellectual property treaties or trade agreements, are some other examples of points of attachment.

Liberty Survives by Mary Atwood © 2009

Animals Need Not Apply

In 2011, nature photographer David Slater left his camera unattended in a Sulawesi wildlife reserve. According to Slater, a Celebes crested macaque named Naruto took the camera, pointed it at himself, posed, clicked the shutter and shot some selfies. The Naruto photos were later published as the *Monkey Selfies* book, which identified Slater and Wildlife Personalities, Ltd. as the copyright owners of the portraits.

People for the Ethical Treatment of Animals ("PETA") as Next Friends of Naruto filed a lawsuit for copyright infringement claiming that Naruto was the author of the photographs he took of himself. The lawsuit was dismissed on the ground that Naruto, an animal, was not eligible to sue for copyright infringement. The 9th Circuit reasoned that references in the Copyright Act to the inheritance rights of children, legitimate or not, grandchildren, and widows of authors necessarily excluded animals who do not marry or have heirs entitled to property by law.

Copy Cat by Mary Atwood © 2022

In 1879, the U.S. Supreme Court stated that "writings" entitled to copyright protection are the fruits of intellectual labor founded in the creative powers of the mind. The U.S. Copyright office relied on this for authority for its consistent refusal to register works attributed to animal authors on this basis. Similarly, works created by nature such as natural stones and driftwood shaped and smoothed by the ocean are also outside the realm of copyright.

Deus ex Machina

God, Brahma, Venus, Zeus, and Maman Brigitte cannot be authors. The U.S. Copyright Office will not register a work purportedly created by divine or supernatural beings. Registration may be allowed if the application or deposit copy simply states that the work was inspired by a divine spirit, but a registration naming the Holy Spirit as the author will be refused.

People not Machines

"Writings" must be the fruits of intellectual labor founded in the creative powers of the mind to be eligible for copyright protection.

Machines cannot be authors. Medical imaging produced by x-rays, ultrasounds, or other diagnostic equipment, and other works produced by a machine or mere mechanical process without creative input are ineligible for copyright. The U.S. Copyright Office will refuse to register a claim in a work that is created through the operation of a machine or process without sufficient human interaction, even if the design is randomly generated.

Robotic Sketch by Mary Atwood © 2018

Artificial Intelligence Is (Not)

AI is not a Terminator automaton or the evil HAL in *2001: A Space Odyssey.* AI is the algorithm, software or hardware that runs self-driving cars, Roomba, Siri, Alexa, your smartphone, DALL-E, Midjourney and ChatGPT, and a myriad of other toys and tools we use every day.

AI is defined by the National Institute of Science and Technology as:

> "(1) A branch of computer science devoted to developing data processing systems that performs functions normally associated with human intelligence, such as reasoning, learning, and self-improvement. (2) The capability of a device to perform functions that are normally associated with human intelligence such as reasoning, learning, and self-improvement."

Margaret Boden, OBE FSA and author of *AI: It's Nature and Future* more simply states, "AI seeks to make computers do the sorts of things minds can do."

BIG Questions and Copyright Issues

The emerging field of AI ethics is grappling with big questions of bias, privacy, transparency, security and safety. Copyright law and technology continue to dance. Copyright scholars, the U.S. Copyright Office professional associations, and lawmakers are figuring out how existing copyright rules should apply to AI's ingestion of images and the copyrightability of work created with the use of AI.

The AI/Copyright issues are covered in this order:

- The Output: The Copyrightability of AI generated works
- The Input: Concerns raised by the use of copyrighted works to train AI
- In and Out: The application of the fair use doctrine to input and output

The Output

AI generated visual art is the product of generative platforms utilizing algorithms to respond to text prompts crafted (for the purposes of this discussion) by a human. This process raises questions that go to the core of copyright law:

- Who is the author of the work? The platform? The human prompter?
- Are AI generated works copyrightable?

Authorship has traditionally required human input in U.S. copyright law. The copyrightability of photographs was initially contested on that basis. That objection was overcome long ago, and photographs are clearly within the realm of copyright protection.

Zarya of the Dawn and The U.S. Copyright Office Answer

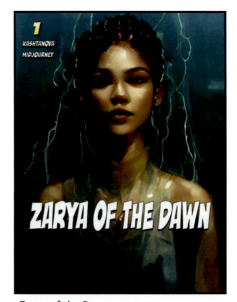

Zarya of the Dawn cover

After Kristina Kashtanova obtained a copyright registration for the text and visual content of the *Zarya of the Dawn* comic book, the U.S. Copyright Office learned of statements on social media that the work was created using artificial intelligence. It notified Kashtanova that the registration would be cancelled unless she could convince them otherwise.

The Copyright Office allowed Kashtanova to retain the copyright for the text she wrote and the selection, coordination, and arrangement of the work's written and visual elements. Kashtanova's position that Midjourney was merely an assistive computer-based tool like Adobe Photoshop was rejected. The vast majority of the Midjourney images were found not to have even the modicum of creativity requisite for copyright protection.

Zarya of the Dawn illustrations, text, and selection example

The Copyright Office explained:

> "Rather than a tool that Ms. Kashtanova controlled and guided to reach her desired image, Midjourney generates images in an unpredictable way. Accordingly, Midjourney users are not the "authors" for copyright purposes of the images the technology generates. As the Supreme Court has explained, the "author" of a copyrighted work is the one "who has actually formed the picture," the one who acts as "the inventive or master mind." Burrow-Giles, 111 U.S. at 61. A person who provides text prompts to Midjourney does not "actually form" the generated images and is not the "master mind" behind them. Instead, as explained above, Midjourney begins the image generation process with a field of visual "noise," which is refined based on tokens created from user prompts that relate to Midjourney's training database. The information in the prompt may "influence" generated image, but prompt text does not dictate a specific result. See Prompts, MIDJOURNEY, https://docs.midjourney.com/docs/prompts (explaining that short text prompts cause "each word [to have] a more powerful influence" and that images including in a prompt may "influence the style and content of the finished result"). Because of the significant distance between what a user may direct Midjourney to create and the visual material Midjourney actually produces, Midjourney users lack sufficient control over generated images to be treated as the "master mind" behind them."

The Copyright Office's denial of registration for lack of human authorship for *"A Recent Entrance to Paradise"* created by a computer algorithm running on a machine" was affirmed by the U.S. District Court for the District of Columbia. Applicant Steven Thaler's argument that his ownership of the machine gave rise to a "work made for hire" was rejected.

The Copyright Office now requires that AI use must be disclosed, detailed, and disclaimed on applications for copyright registration. Works that contain sufficient human input are eligible for registration.

How Much is Enough?

Jason Allen's input of at least 624 revisions and text prompts and alteration with Adobe Photoshop to create his award-winning image, *Theatre D'opera Spatial,* with the use of Midjourney was not enough. His application was rejected because it was not the product of human authorship.

Some OBVIOUSly Different Answers

Obvious, a French collective of artists, researchers and friends, are exploring the creative potential of artificial intelligence. Obvious was behind one of the first big AI works to impact the art world when its portrait of Edmond de Belamy created by a Generative Adversarial Network was auctioned at Christies for $432,500.00 in 2018. The portrait is signed by the algorithm used to create it.

We interviewed Obvious about the copyrightability of their work. They believe there will always be a human algorithm. An algorithm data selection would follow the indications of the human that coded it.

Edmond de Belamy, from La Famille de Belamy by Obvious

Obvious told us "We actually started working with algorithms that aim at replicating creativity because we were fascinated by this question. We don't totally understand creativity and our position is that if we can better understand it by trying to replicate it using artificial intelligence. Today we are able to replicate part of it. Especially, the "learning through example" part. The algorithms we use are said to be inventive according to their creator, as they are capable of creating unique and new visuals, which are components of creativity. Nevertheless, we are still unable to make algorithms understand notions such as usefulness or intention. Therefore, creativity is, for now, still a feature exclusive to humans."

The UK takes a similar approach. The UK's intellectual property law is considered by many to be at the forefront of innovation. It affords copyright protection to computer-generated works. The author of a computer-generated work is the person who made the arrangements for the work to be created.

Karla Saldana Ochoa, the leading researcher at SHARE Lab, a developer of human-centered AI design practices and Urban AI advisor, argues that use of AI in the design process results in a co-authorship between the creators of the algorithm, the creators of the training data and the designer using the AI.

Input: What feeds AI? Does it Infringe Copyrights?

Generative AI needs a lot of input for machine learning. Millions of images are input into AI programs as training material for AI to learn to match words with images. The images are often obtained by "scraping."

Scraping (a.k.a. web harvesting, web data extraction, and screen scraping) is a process used to extract copious amounts of content, images, and other data from websites. There is an anti-scraping outcry. The rallying cry "Consent, Credit, Compensation" demands that artists and other content creators retain control of their work and be credited and compensated for its use.

Legislators and industry group panels abound. Lawsuits by illustrators and others claiming that scraping is infringement of the artist's vested rights to copy, distribute and make derivative works are in the early stages of litigation.

License to Train

Copyright owners have begun to offer AI training licenses which permit copying for a fee. Many developers have not been paying license fees. This negatively impacts the market for copyright owners to license work for AI training data sets.

Q: Fair Use?

A: It Depends

Fair use is the right to use copyrighted material without payment or permission in some circumstances. It is often asserted as a defense against copyright infringement. Here is quick look at what "it depends" on and how successfully, or not, the defense may fare in the use of copyrighted material for AI training.

	Fair Use Factors + *AI Facts*
	The purpose and character of the work including whether such use is of a commercial nature or is for nonprofit educational purposes. *The use of images to train AI platforms is almost always commercial. Whether it can be classified as transformative or not is a wide open question.*
	The nature of the copyrighted work. *The more creative the work being ingested, the more this factor weighs against fair use.*
	The amount and substantiality of the portion used in relation to the copyrighted work as a whole. *The entire work is usually copied. This weighs against fair use but is not determinative. This may be offset if the entire work is not later shared.*
	The effect of the use upon the potential market for or value of the copyrighted work. *Use of the copyrighted work without payment or permission would likely impact the market for the copyrighted work negatively.*

As always, fair use is always a fact specific inquiry that must be made on a case-by-case basis.

Moving Forward

AI technologies will continue to change. Its use will likely continue to expand exponentially. Copyright law will continue to follow and respond. To follow the exciting evolution of this pairing, you can sign up for Copyright Alliance's AI Copyright Alert at https://copyrightalliance.org/get-involved/ai-copyright-alert/.

Collaborations, Co-Authors, Commissions, and Compilations

Collaborate by Deborah Reid © 2023

Andy Warhol and Jean-Michel Basquiat, Auguste Rodin and Camille Claudel, Christo and Jeane-Claude, Lee Miller and Man Ray, Marina Abramovic and Ulay Laysiepen, Claes Oldenberg and Coosje van Bruggen, Rogers and Hammerstein, Simon and Garfunkel, the Beatles . . . . . The list goes on.

Collaborations have yielded rich results through the ages. Collaborations have also led to a lot of lawsuits and ruptured relationships. Co-authors are co-owners of the copyright. If a work is profitable, the stakes and potential payoff of being classified as a co-author are high.

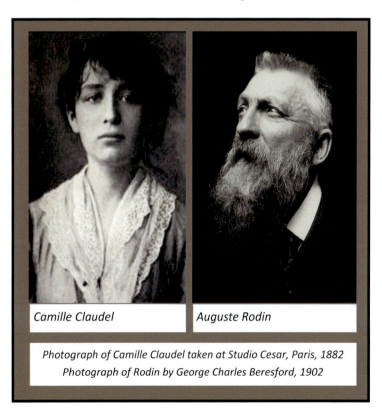

Camille Claudel | *Auguste Rodin*

Photograph of Camille Claudel taken at Studio Cesar, Paris, 1882
Photograph of Rodin by George Charles Beresford, 1902

An understanding of who qualifies as a co-author and the resulting consequences can help to manage expectations and avoid the quagmires of litigation. It can enable you to create amazing works with your fellow artists and keep your relationships intact.

The Statutory Framework

The Copyright Act provides:

> "Copyright ownership vests initially in the author or **authors** of the work."

> "The **authors** of a **joint work** are the **co-owners** of copyright in the work."

Simple.

Defining Lines

It gets more complicated.

A joint work is defined as:

> "A **joint work** is a work prepared by two or more **authors** with the intention that their contributions be merged into inseparable or interdependent parts of a unitary whole." (Emphasis added)

The terms joint author and co-author are equivalents and are used interchangeably.

Although most types of creative contributions can qualify for joint authorship, not all contributors to a work are joint authors. Generally, technical roles like editors, sound engineers, secretaries, draftsmen, research assistants, colleagues with helpful comments do not qualify as joint or co-authors.

The incentive to be classified as a co-author of a lucrative work is strong. Co-authors are co-owners of the copyright and are entitled to share in the profits.

To draw the line between who is and who is not a co-author, the courts examine:

- The intent of the parties
- The nature of the contribution

Not all courts draw the line in the same place.

Intent: To Be, or Not to Be, a Co-Author

The intent of collaborators to be co-authors is a key element of a joint work. The collaborators must intend for their contributions to be merged into a single copyrightable work. The contributions must be either inseparable or interdependent.

If there is no agreement, the courts will look to industry standards, communications between the parties, and how they describe the work to others, to determine what their intent was. This can lead to complications.

No matter how well you mesh artistically with your collaborator, you probably cannot read his or her mind. Minds change over time. A simple agreement can avoid having courts decide what you wanted for you, manage expectations, and preserve friendships.

Nature of the Contribution: Copyrightable, or Not

Here is where the law gets a little complicated: There is a minority rule, and a majority rule, and an exception to the majority rule.

- First, the minority rule. Some circuits require only that the whole work, not the contributions to the work, be copyrightable.
- Next, the majority rule. Most circuits, including the influential 2nd and 9th Circuits, require that each author's contribution be independently copyrightable for an author to qualify as a co-author.
- Now, the exception to the majority rule. The 7th Circuit has carved out an exception to the majority rule. Where the contributions could not stand alone, due to the creative process used to produce the work, they do not have to be copyrightable on their own.

The rationale for this exception is that it would be paradoxical if, through the joint labor, a work was created that had enough originality to be copyrighted, but due to the division of labor, no contributor could claim a copyright.

Now a story that illustrates how the rules played out.

A Comic Book Case Study

Todd McFarlane, a writer, illustrator, and publisher, and Neil Gaiman, a script writer, are both celebrities in the comic book world.

In 1992, McFarlane wrote, illustrated, and began publishing the *Spawn* series. After early issues were criticized for bad writing, McFarlane invited top writers to pen scripts for *Spawn*.

Gaiman accepted the invitation. Beyond McFarlane's assurance that he would treat Gaiman "better than the big guys did", there was no discussion of compensation or copyright.

In his script of *Spawn No. 9*, Gaiman introduced three new characters; Angela, Count Nicholas Cogliostro, and Medieval Spawn. Gaiman provided the names for Angela and the Count. He described and wrote the dialogue for all three. The characters were all drawn by McFarlane.

Spawn No. 9 was a huge success. It sold more than a million copies. McFarlane paid Gaiman $100,000.00 about what Gaiman would have

Judging the Spawn by Mary Atwood © 2023

expected to receive from one of the "big guys" for a script. McFarlane later paid Gaiman approximately $30,000.00 to create a three-part Angela mini-series and $20,000.00 as royalties on a Medieval Spawn action figure.

In 1996, Gaiman learned that McFarlane might sell his enterprise and decided he needed the protection of a written contract. Contract negotiations failed.

Gaiman filed suit asking for a declaration that he was the co-owner of the copyrights for Angela, Cogliostro, and Medieval Spawn. McFarlane conceded Gaiman's co-ownership of Angela.

Co-Ownership of the Count

McFarlane asked Gaiman to include a wizened sage character to provide background information and move the story along. In a draft, Gaiman described "a really old bum, a skinny, balding, old man with a greyish-yellow beard, like a skinny Santa Claus" who displayed mysterious wisdom and called himself Count Nicholas Cogliostro. The Count was drawn by McFarlane as an old man with a long grey beard who faintly resembled Moses instead.

McFarlane argued that his drawings, not Gaiman's writing, were what made Cogliostro copyrightable. He contended that Gaiman contributed only the non-copyrightable stock character of a drunken old bum.

The court disagreed. Cogliostro's name, age, phony title, what he knew and said, and faintly biblical facial features were written in by Gaiman and created a distinctive character. The court explained that although Gaiman's contribution might not have been copyrightable in and of itself, it added expressive content which transformed Cogliostro from a mere drawing to a comic-book character who was the joint work of Gaiman and McFarlane.

Medieval Spawn

Medieval Spawn was a closer case. The original Spawn, created by McFarlane, was a tall figure with a shiny plastic oval for a face, clad in a neural parasite and a huge red cape. Gaiman's script for *Spawn No. 9* opened with a different Spawn, dressed as a knight from the Middle Ages astride a huge horse.

Gaiman's contributions were analyzed through the lens of derivative works. The court found that his addition of a knight's costume and medieval speech made Medieval Spawn sufficiently distinct from the original Spawn to qualify as a derivative work. These additions also satisfied the copyrightable requirement for joint authorship.

The Consequences of Co-Authorship

Co-authors are co-owners of the copyright in a joint work. They each have equal rights to register and enforce the copyright.

Absent an agreement to the contrary, each joint author has the equal right to exercise each of the exclusive rights in the copyright bundle.

Each co-author may distribute the work and make derivative works without the consent of the other co-author(s). Each co-author may independently grant nonexclusive licenses in and to an entire joint work without the consent of the other co-author(s). Each joint author could potentially grant the same type of non-exclusive licenses to competing third parties. Not an optimal situation.

Co-authors' rights are subject only to a duty to account for and share the profits equally. That's right – equally.

Absent an agreement to the contrary, profits are divided equally among the co-authors. The share of the profits is not commensurate with the amount of work or effort contributed.

Don't be "absent an agreement".

Royalties are Different

A co-author's right to share in the profits of a work are not the same thing as being entitled to receive royalties from a publisher. Royalties are compensation paid to the owner of a copyright or other intellectual property for the right to use or profit from the property. Royalties are often a percentage of sales. For example, an artist may be paid an agreed upon percentage of all sales of a print. The percentage is a matter of contract, not a matter of copyright law.

Royalty is Different by Mary Atwood © 2018

Works Made for Hire

What are Works Made For Hire?

'Work made for hire' is a term that is used widely and often incorrectly. There are two mutually exclusive situations in which works made for hire are produced:

1. The work is created by an employee in the scope of employment.

OR

2. The work falls into one of the 9 categories of work allowed by the Copyright Act AND it was created as a result of express written agreement between the creator of the work and a person specially ordering or commissioning it.

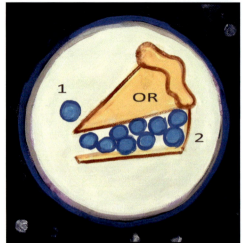

1 or 2 by Deborah Reid © 2022

Classification as work made for hire, or not, is consequential. Unlike other works, copyright in works made for hire is not owned by the person that created the work. The copyright in a work made for hire is owned by an employer or the entity that ordered the work. There are other important consequences.

But first, the first situation.

Works Created by Employees in the Scope of Employment

The first step to figure out whether there is work made for hire is to determine whether the work was prepared by an employee or an independent contractor. Here are some examples of questions courts ask to make this determination:

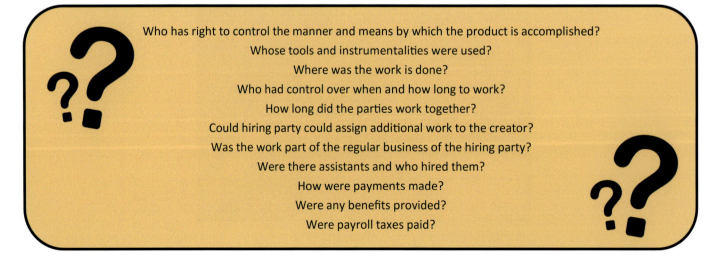

- Who has right to control the manner and means by which the product is accomplished?
- Whose tools and instrumentalities were used?
- Where was the work is done?
- Who had control over when and how long to work?
- How long did the parties work together?
- Could hiring party could assign additional work to the creator?
- Was the work part of the regular business of the hiring party?
- Were there assistants and who hired them?
- How were payments made?
- Were any benefits provided?
- Were payroll taxes paid?

The Supreme Court posed these questions to determine whether the *Third World America* sculpture by James Earl Reid was a work made for hire. The Community for Creative Non-Violence (CCNV) hired Reid to turn its idea – a modern Nativity scene of a contemporary homeless family huddled on a steam grate – into a sculpture. CCNV inspected and directed the sculpture while in progress to ensure its specifications would be met.

Reid was a sculptor, a skilled occupation. Reid supplied his own tools, worked in his own studio, set his own hours and hired his own assistants. The singular project took less than two months.

Heart of Stone by Mary Atwood © 2022

CCNV was not in the business of creating sculptures. It did not pay payroll or Social Security taxes, provide employee benefits, or contribute to unemployment insurance or workers' compensation funds.

All factors, except CCNV's control over final product details, supported the determination that Reid was not an employee. The court quickly found that the sculpture did not fit in any of 9 categories of specially commissioned works that can be works made for hire. *Third World America* was not a work made for hire.

The Supreme Court left open the question of whether CCNV's creative input and final product control made CCNV a joint author. This open question and the lengthy, expensive trip up to the Supreme Court could have been avoided by use of a well-crafted contract.

The Second Situation

One of the most common misconceptions about intellectual property is that a commissioning party automatically owns the copyright in the commissioned work. Not true.

For copyright ownership to vest in the commissioning party, there must be an agreement stating that the work is a work made for hire AND the work is one the nine types listed in the Copyright Act.

Other kinds of work, even if specially ordered or commissioned, cannot be works made for hire. Copyright ownership in those works can be transferred from the author by an assignment or contract.

Here is the list of the types of works with a bit of amplification for a few of the more technical terms:

Works Specially Ordered or Commission for Use as:

1. Contribution to Collective Works
Independent works that are assembled into a collective whole. Magazines, anthologies and encyclopedias are collective works. Individual articles, stories or essays are contributions to collective works.

2. Part of a Motion Picture or Audiovisual Work
An audiovisual work is a series of related images and accompanying sounds (intrinsically) intended to be shown by use of machines or devices. A motion picture is an audiovisual work of related images that when shown in succession impart an impression of motion.
Soundtracks, screenplays, costumes and set design can be parts of motion pictures and other audiovisual works.

3. A Translation

4. A Supplementary Work
A secondary adjunct to a work by another author to amplify or comment on the initial work. Forewords, pictorial illustrations, maps, charts, bibliographies and indexes are examples.

5. A Compilation
A work formed by the collection and assembling of preexisting material in such a way that the resulting whole constitutes an original work of authorship.

6. An Instructional Text
A work to be used in systematic instructional activities. Instructional texts can be literary, pictorial or graphic.

7. A Test

8. Answer Material for a Test

9. An Atlas

There Are Consequences

There are consequences. Important consequences. Unlike other kinds of works, the author of a work made for hire is not the person who created the work. The author of a work made for hire is the employer. This is important.

The author owns the copyright. The author holds all the rights in the exclusive bundle. The author can sell, assign, divide, subdivide and license any of these rights. The creator of a work made for hire cannot.

A party that specially commissions a work is not the author and does not own the copyright unless the specific requirements of a work made for hire are met. This is also consequential. For example, absent a written agreement providing that a video you commissioned to promote your business, the videographer, not you, will own the copyright in the video.

The life span and availability of termination rights are different for works made for hire. Copyrights in works made for hire last for 95 years from the date of publication or 120 years from the date of creation whichever comes first. Copyright protection for other works is the life of the author plus 70 years. The copyright term for works made for hire usually works out to be shorter. Termination rights available to authors or their heirs in certain circumstance do not apply to works made for hire. Works made for hire carry no VARA rights.

7 Q by Mary Atwood © 2023

When you understand what works made for hire are, you can avoid some thorny problems. To sort out whether a particular piece is a work made for hire or not, ask the questions in the next section, 7 Questions.

7 Questions

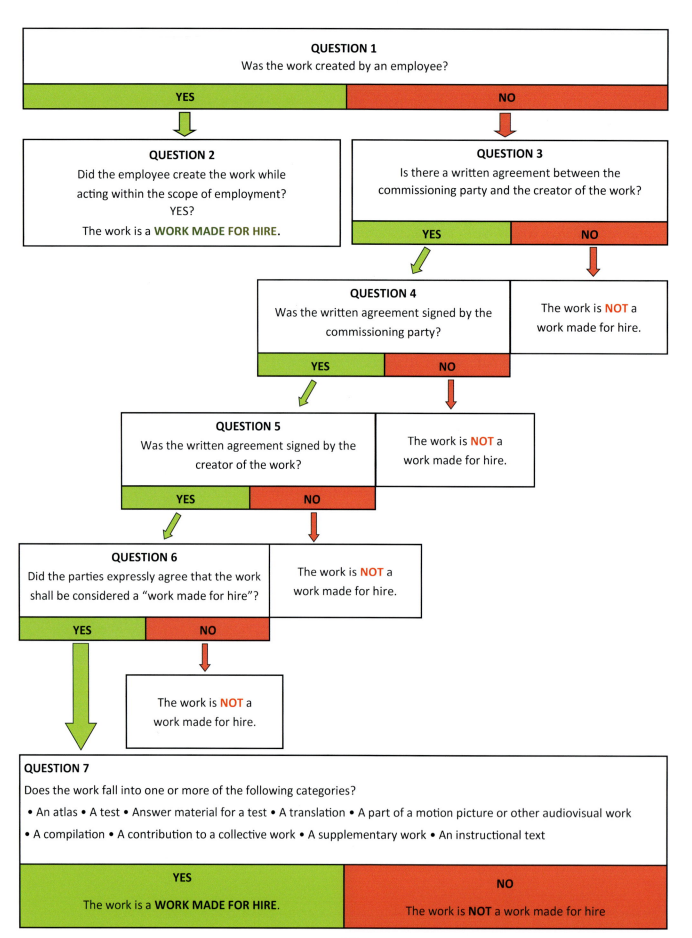

Assignments and Transfers

Introduction

Copyright is an intellectual property right separate from the copyrighted work itself. The copyright is retained by the author even when the work itself is sold.

For example, when a photographer sells a photograph, the purchaser gets the actual physical print. The purchaser can hang it in his living room, put it in a closet, give it away, or sell it to someone else. The sale of the work does not transfer the copyright.

The photographer, not the purchaser, keeps the copyright and can make reproductions or exercise any of the other rights in the exclusive bundle. The photographer can also transfer the copyright itself to others.

Copyrights can be bought, sold, divided, subdivided, transferred, assigned, or licensed. Copyright owners often transfer portions of their exclusive rights to book publishers, record companies, distributors, and others who can get the copyrighted work to the market. Assignments and licenses are two common vehicles for copyright transfer.

What is an Assignment?

Assignments are a way to transfer intellectual property ownership. The copyright owner is referred to as the 'assignor". The assignor legally transfers "all right, title and interest" in a copyright to another, the assignee. The assignor has no control, the assignee can do whatever it wants.

Assignments must be in writing. Agreements for commissioned works often provide for assignment of all the intellectual property in the work to the person commissioning the work (a.k.a. the assignee). Even in specially commissioned works that clearly qualify as works made for hire, it is good practice to include an assignment clause.

Licenses

Why Use a License?

If you want to maintain control of your copyright use a license, not an assignment. Assignments transfer ownership and relinquish control to the assignee.

Licenses do not transfer ownership. Licenses permit someone to use your copyrighted work according to the terms of the license.

Different kinds of driver's licenses permit you to do different things like drive a car, ride a motorcycle or drive a bus.

Different kinds of copyright licenses give permission to do different things. The uses you permit can be limited.

Pandemic Plate by Deborah Reid © 2020

License This, License That

The right to use copyrighted material can be divided and subdivided into smaller permissions almost endlessly. Just like license plates, you can customize copyright licenses to permit the rights you want to allow.

Here is a menu of some of the basic choices to consider in building your license.

THIS?	OR	THAT?
Exclusive?	OR	Non-Exclusive ?
Everywhere?	OR	Only in some geographic areas?
What media?	OR	All or some?
Forever?	OR	For a limited period of time?
For free?	OR	How much will you be paid?
Revocable?	OR	Irrevocable?

How to Create a License

There are three ways to create a license:

- by a written agreement
- by an oral agreement
- by the parties' behavior

Only exclusive licenses, like assignments, must be in writing. Oral agreements for non-exclusive licenses are enforceable. Where there is no actual agreement, courts may find and enforce implied licenses based on the surrounding circumstances. This is a circumstance you want to avoid.

By Implication

Implied licenses are created when one party:

- creates a work at another person's request
- delivers the work to that person
- and intends that the person copy and distribute the work

Implied licenses can be limited to specific uses IF that limitation is expressly conveyed when the work is delivered.

It is always better to articulate your intentions than to have a court determine what your conduct meant in retrospect. Courts may well allow more uses than you intended.

The 11th Circuit found that an artist's delivery of a painted motorcycle to Roaring Toyz, a company specializing in custom motorcycles, also allowed Kawasaki, the motorcycle manufacturer, to feature the painted bike in its advertising.

Another court found that a photographer hired by another photographer to shoot an event involving a Real Housewife of Atlanta gave the event manager an implied license to use the photographs on social media and to sell publication rights to *People* magazine.

CAVEAT CREATOR • ARTIST BEWARE

Moral of the Story: Make your own license. Write it down. Don't let a court write your story.

CopyLEFT

The copyleft movement is on a mission to provide alternatives to copyright. Copyright is "all rights reserved". Copyleft is an alternative, or "some rights reserved".

In 1989, GNU created the first version of the copyleft open source license for software. Open source licensed software programs are free and require that all modified and extended versions of the program are free.

Shepard Fairey created this logo for the 20th anniversary of Creative Commons. It is included in this book pursuant to a C BY license.

Creative Commons

In 2002, Creative Commons developed a set of licenses to further its mission to "overcome legal obstacles to the sharing of knowledge and creativity". The Creative Commons (CC) licenses provide a simple, standardized way to grant copyright permissions for creative work.

The CC licenses have created a vast digital pool of cultural content, historic images, scientific articles, photos, videos and more that can be copied, distribute, edited, remixed and/or built upon. You have probably already agreed to CC licenses. CC licenses are used on Wikipedia, Flickr and YouTube.

The growing digital commons spans 86 countries and includes over two billion works. It is much like the public domain with some limitations on use.

3 Things, 4 Components, and 6+ Licenses

Three important things to know about all Creative Commons licenses:

1. The licenses are free for all to use without compensation to Creative Commons.

2. The licenses all permit use of the work by anyone without payment to the author.

3. All of the licenses require attribution to the author. Five of the six licenses have more requirements.

These are the four components used to build the licenses:

1. **BY** - attribution required.
2. **NC** - no commercial use.
3. **ND** - no derivative works.
4. **SA** - Share Alike - the license must be the same on any derivative works.

You cannot not use ND and SA together. SA only applies to derivative works and ND means no derivative works.

The Creative Commons (CC) licenses are:

License Designation + Name	Features
CC BY Attribution	BY = Attribution, is the only requirement of this licenses. Distribution, remixes and adaptions for commercial use (or not) are allowed
CC BY-SA Attribution + Share Alike	In addition to attribution all new works must be licensed under the same terms. i.e., Share Alike.
CC BY-NC	Non-commercial uses with attribution are permitted.
CC BY-NC-SA	Same as above with additional requirements that works licensed under it and derivatives created from it can only be used non-commercially.
CC BY-ND	Again, attribution. Creation of derivative works is prohibited
CC BY NC-ND	No commercial use, no derivatives. Attribution.

And not really a license:

CC Zero	No attribution. No requirements. Not really a license. It is a dedication to the public domain.

Go to www.creativecommons.org for complete and accessible guide on how to use Creative Commons licenses.

It is Forever, for Some

Think about the future before deciding to use a Creative Commons license. If you distribute work under a CC license to create a buzz and then plan to cash in later, think hard. CC licenses are irrevocable, for some.

Although you can stop distribution under a CC license, the CC license terms still apply to people who have already received the content. These recipients can continue to use and share the work under the CC license terms. Wikimedia Commons and other distribution hubs that received content under a CC license may refuse later requests to take content down. The CC license, for them, is forever.

CAVEAT CREATOR ♦ ARTIST BEWARE

The FAIR USE Doctrine

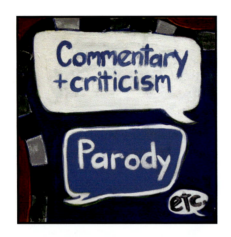
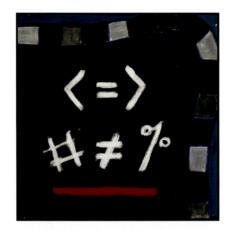
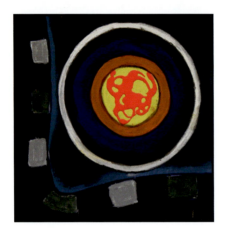

Fair Use is the right to use copyrighted material
without payment or permission in some circumstances.

THE FAIR USE DOCTRINE

A Fair Use Tale

1741: The Origin Story ♦ 1841: Fair Abridgement Comes to the U.S. ♦ 1976: Fair Use Codified
1990: Toward a Standard Standard ♦ 1994: Pretty/Nasty Transformation
2021: Round Peg, Square Hole. No Locks.

Fair Use, the Statute

The Four Statutory Factors

The First Factor

Making Fun ♦ Money Isn't Everything ♦ Warhol v. Goldsmith ♦ Transformative, For Example

The Second Factor

Core Strength ♦ (Un)Published? ♦ Secondary Role

The Third Factor

No Formula—Really ♦ The Heart of the Matter ♦ The Whole Thing

The Fourth Factor

Pictures, Purposes and Profit ♦ Go-to-Market ♦ Do Not Pass Go! ♦ Criticism is Encouraged

All Together Now!

Four More (Stories NOT Factors) ♦ That's Not Fair ♦ Fair Enough

A Fair Use Tale

Once upon a time, books were written by hand. It took a long time. Books were also copied by hand. It also took a long time. Surreptitious copying was not a problem.

In 1440 the world changed. Gutenberg invented the printing press. Multiple copies of books could be printed easily. Surreptitious copying became a problem.

In 1710 the Statute of Anne, the first copyright law, was enacted in Great Britain to address the problem.

1741: The Origin Story

In 1741 the doctrine of fair use, originally known as fair abridgment, was first formulated by an English court in the case of *Gyles v. Wilcox*.

Philip Yorke, 1st Earl of Hardwicke by Michael Dahl

Abridgement, the process of making, shortening or abstracting long texts, was common practice in the 16th century.

Gyles, the publisher of a lengthy legal tome, *Pleas of the Crown*, was not pleased when Wilcox, Barrow and Nutt, ("Wilcox") another publisher, abridged his book and retitled it as *Modern Crown Law*. Gyles filed suit claiming that Wilcox infringed his rights under the Statute of Anne.

The initial book published by Gyles was 275 pages. The allegedly infringing work published by Wilcox was only 35 pages. Wilcox argued that only entire and exact copies were infringements.

Lord Hardwicke, the presiding judge, disagreed. He viewed the Statute of Anne as an act to promote public education and good, not publishing monopolies.

In his seminal opinion, Lord Hardwicke framed this query:

> "When Complaints of this Sort have come before the Court, the single Question has constantly been, Whether the second Book has been the same Book with the former? And where the second Book has not otherwise differ'd from the former than by reducing or shortening the Stile, or by leaving out some of the Words of the first Book, the second Book has been construed the same with the former. But where the second Book has been an abridgment of the former, it has been understood not to be the same Book, and therefore to be out of the Act." . . and "Whether the second Book is the same Book with the former is a Matter of Fact, and a Fact of Difficulty to be determined."

The experts assigned by the court to compare the two texts found that the abridgement was, in fact, fair. The ensuing line of English fair abridgment cases utilized analytical tools remarkably similar to the fair use factors codified in the U.S. Copyright Act of 1976 and currently employed by U.S. Courts.

1841: Fair Abridgement Comes to the U.S.

Copyright law in the United States starts with the U.S. Constitution, which authorizes the legislature to "To promote the progress of science and useful arts, by securing for limited times to authors and inventors the exclusive right to their respective writings and discoveries". In 1790, the first copyright law was signed by President George Washington. It afforded protection to books, maps and charts. George Washington also played a role in the first U.S. fair use case.

Folsom published *The Writings of George Washington,* a twelve-volume compilation with commentary. Marsh later published *The Life of Washington,* a two volume work.

Judge Story, citing English fair abridgement cases, ruled that Marsh's mere selection, different arrangement and the *"facile use of scissors"* were simply a studied evasion and not a fair abridgment.

1976: Fair Use Codified

In 1976, the fair use doctrine became a statute. The statute provides that the fair use of a copyrighted work is not an infringement of copyright. The factors developed by the courts in over 200 years of litigation are laid out as non-exclusive guidelines in Section 106 of the 1976 Copyright Act.

The 4 Fair Use Factors are:

- The purpose and character of the second work - the potentially infringing work

The Athenaeum Portrait by Gilbert Stuart

- The nature of the first work – the original work that was used in the second work

- The amount and substantiality of the first work used in the second work

- The impact on the market for the first work

The statute anticipates that the doctrine will be continued to be developed by the courts on a case by case basis. The case by case basis application of the factors initially yielded widely disparate results.

1990: Toward a Standard Standard

Important publishers and entertainment industry players are located in the jurisdiction of the U.S. District Court for the Southern District of New York. It hears a substantial percentage of important copyright cases.

By the luck of the draw, Judge Pierre N. Leval was assigned a fair number of cases involving copyright infringement and fair use. Some of his decisions were appealed and some were overturned. This spurred Judge Leval on to become a leading legal scholar on the fair use doctrine. In 1993, his influential commentary *Toward a Fair Use Standard* was published by the Harvard Law Review. The commentary examined the history and goals of copyright in general and fair use in particular, and demonstrated the consistency of their objectives. As Judge Leval stated:

> "The stimulation of creative thought and authorship for the benefit of society depends assuredly on the protection of the author's monopoly. But it depends equally on the recognition that the monopoly must have limits. Those limits include the public dedication of facts (not withstanding the author's efforts in uncovering them), the public dedication of ideas (not withstanding the author's creation) and the public dedication of the right to make fair use of material covered by the copyright."

In sum, the purpose of both copyright and the fair use doctrine are the same: the enrichment of public knowledge. Copyright does so by providing monopoly rights to authors to incentivize them to share work. Fair use does so by providing protection to transformative secondary creativity.

Judge Leval's commentary was referenced by the Supreme Court several times in the landmark fair use case of *Campbell v. Acuff Rose Music, Inc.*

1994: Pretty/Nasty Transformation

Acuff-Rose Music, Inc. was the registered owner of the copyright of Roy Orbison's 1964 hit, *Oh, Pretty Woman*. Luther R. Campbell, a member of 2 Live Crew, later penned lyrics for a second version, *Pretty Woman*. Unlike the original rock ballad which used the "Pretty Woman" refrain consistently, 2 Live Crew's rap rendition progressed from Pretty Woman to Nasty Woman, Big Hairy Woman, Bald Headed Woman and Two Timin' Woman.

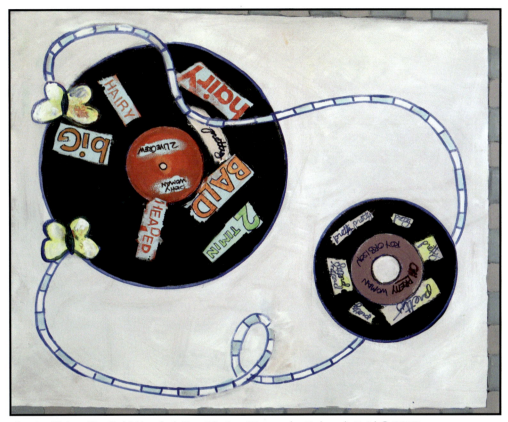

Pretty, Hairy, Big, Bald Headed, Two Timing Woman by Deborah Reid © 2019

2 Live Crew's offer to pay Acuff-Rose to license the song was refused. 2 Live Crew recorded their version anyway. One year and 250,000 copies later, Acuff-Rose sued for copyright infringement.

The lower courts found that the 2 Live Crew version was an infringement based in large part on the fact that it was commercial use. The U.S. Supreme Court disagreed.

It applied the four statutory factors. It held the commercial nature of 2 Live Crew's work was not dispositive. It determined that 2 Live Crew's version was a fair use because it was a parody that did not usurp the market for the original. It was in their words "transformative".

2021: Round Peg, Square Hole. No Locks.

Parisian Love Locks by Mary Atwood © 2012

Some judges have complained that "applying copyright law to computer programs is like assembling a jigsaw puzzle whose pieces do not quite fit". In *Google v. Oracle,* the Supreme Court retrofitted fair use to computer code.

Oracle owned the JAVA SE platform. Programmers use the popular Java language to write programs able to run on any desktop or laptop regardless of the underlying hardware. Oracle made it freely available to software and app developers but not to competitors.

Google, without permission, copied the Java interface declaring code for use in its Android operating system to allow programmers to use the familiar coding language. Not surprisingly, Oracle sued. Google asserted a fair use defense. After years of litigation, the case made its way to the Supreme Court.

At the outset, the Supreme Court noted that unlike many other copyrightable works, computer programs almost always serve functional purposes. Useful articles are generally beyond the scope of copyright protection.

The Supreme Court conducted the four factor fair use analysis starting with the second factor – the factor most closely aligned with the issue of copyrightability. It focused on the purpose of copyright and how enforcing a copyright for Oracle would be at odds with the enrichment of public knowledge. The Java API declaring code would become a lock to which only Oracle had the key. The flow of creative improvements, new applications and uses that could be developed by users already fluent in Java would be blocked.

The Supreme Court held that Google's use was a fair use. In closing, the Supreme Court specifically stated that the nature of fair use concepts had not changed and that the case did not "overturn or modify our earlier cases involving fair use—cases, for example, which involve "knockoff" products, journalistic writings, and parodies."

The Supreme Court next considered the fair use doctrine in the eagerly anticipated art world case of *The Andy Warhol Foundation v. Goldsmith.* Its consideration was limited to an exploration, application and amplification of the first fair use factor – the purpose and character of the potentially infringing use. In other words, did Warhol's silk screen *Orange Prince* created from Goldsmith's black and white portrait have a different purpose or character than the original photograph? The answer: It depends how *Orange Prince* is used. A less cryptic answer and deeper dive into the case is presented in The First Factor, just ahead.

Puzzles by Deborah Reid © 2020

Fair Use, The Statute

The factors developed by the courts in over 200 years of litigation to figure out whether or not a use was fair were codified in the U.S. Copyright Act of 1976. The statute itself is illuminating.

First, we will parse out the preamble. We will then list and analyze the factors, and tell stories of their application in actual cases.

On to the preamble:

> Notwithstanding the provisions of sections 106 and 106A,
>
> the **fair use** of a **copyrighted work**,
>
> including such **use by reproduction** in copies or phonorecords **or by any other means** specified by that section,
>
> for **purposes** such as
>
> **criticism, comment,**
>
> **news reporting, teaching**
> (including multiple copies for classroom use),
>
> **scholarship,**
>
> or **research,**
>
> is **not** an **infringement** of **copyright.**

Fair use is an affirmative defense to copyright infringement. An affirmative defense is a new fact or set of facts that defeat a claim even if facts supporting a claim are true. If you assert the affirmative defense of fair use, you are saying " I copied it and I am allowed to." A statute of limitations is also an affirmative defense. If you assert a statute of limitations defense, you are saying "So what if I did. It's too late to sue me."

The Four Statutory Factors

To determine whether a use of copyrighted work is a "fair use" and therefore allowable, the courts look at the particular facts of each case and apply the four factors laid out in the statute.

The four factors are:

1.		the **purpose and character of the use,** including whether such use is of a **commercial** nature or is for **nonprofit educational** purposes;
2.		the **nature** of the **copyrighted work**;
3.		the **amount and substantiality** of the portion **used** in relation to the **copyrighted work** as a whole; and
4.		the **effect of the use** upon the **potential market** for or value of the **copyrighted work**.

Each of the factors will be discussed individually, but first a few points about how they work in general.

- The factors are not exclusive.
- The factors are to be weighed together.
- Historically, but not always, the first and fourth factors have been given the greatest weight.

There are no bright line rules. Fair use determinations are made by open-ended, context sensitive, case-by case inquiries.

The ultimate question "is whether copyright law's goal of promoting the Progress of Science and useful Arts would be better served by allowing the use than by preventing it."

The Weight by Mary Atwood and Deborah Reid © 2023

Blurry by Deborah Reid © 2019

The First Factor

The first factor is:

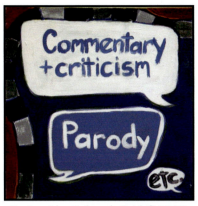

Factor 1 by Deborah Reid © 2019

(1) the **purpose and character of the use**,

including whether such **use** is

of a **commercial** nature

or is for **nonprofit educational** purposes.

This factor focuses on the allegedly infringing work – "the use". It examines whether the use has a further purpose or a different character than the original. If the new use conveys a new expression, meaning or message this factor favors fair use.

Original copyrightable expressions used as raw material, transformed to create new information, aesthetics, insights and understandings are at the core of fair use protection.

Making Fun

A parody is a "composition in prose or verse in which the characteristic turns of thought and phrase in an author or class of authors are imitated in such a way as to make them appear ridiculous."

"Parody needs to mimic an original to make its point, and so has some claim to use the creation of its victim's imagination."

Parody is a good example of the type of use that can convey a new message. Like more serious forms of criticism, parodies can provide social benefit, by shedding light on an earlier work, and, in the process, creating a new one.

Scholarship, research, criticism, comment, news reporting and teaching are also good examples of uses that often—but not always – convey new expressions, meanings or messages.

Money Isn't Everything

An evaluation of the first fair use factor also takes into account whether the use of the work is of a commercial nature or is for non-profit educational purposes.

Use for non-profit educational purposes can be unfair. The educational text publishing industry would go out of business if educational texts could be widely used without restriction or compensation.

Commercial uses can be fair uses. Criticism, commentary, research and news reporting have at least two things in common. They are listed in the preamble to the fair use statute as the type of uses that are often fair uses AND they are all uses that are often done commercially.

Money on the Table by Deborah Reid © 2019

Bad faith, like commerciality, becomes less relevant the more transformative the use. Many courts and scholars take the position that it should not even be considered.

Warhol v. Goldsmith

In *Andy Warhol Foundation vs. Goldsmith,* the Supreme Court expounded on the first fair use factor. First, the facts of the case. Then the issue, the majority ruling and analysis, brief summaries of the concurring and dissenting opinions.

The Facts

Andy Warhol is well known for his images of celebrities like Marilyn Monroe and products like Campbell's soup cans. His works appear in museums around the world. His contribution to modern art is undeniable.

Lynn Goldsmith began her career in rock and roll photography when there were few women in the genre. Her subjects included Bob Dylan, Mick Jagger, Patti Smith, Bruce Springsteen, Led Zeppelin, and James Brown. Her award winning photographs appeared in *Life*, *Time*, *Rolling Stone*, and *People* magazines, as well as the National Portrait Gallery and the Museum of Modern Art.

In 1981, *Newsweek* commissioned Goldsmith to photograph an up and coming musician, Prince Rogers Nelson. One of the photographs was published by *Newsweek* along with an article about Prince. Another of Goldsmith's studio photographs, a black and white portrait, is the original copyrighted work at issue.

In 1984, Goldsmith granted a limited one-time only license to *Vanity Fair* to use her black and white portrait as an artist reference for a magazine illustration. *Vanity Fair* paid Goldsmith a $400.00 license fee. *Vanity Fair* then paid Andy Warhol an undisclosed amount to create the illustration. Andy Warhol used Goldsmith's photograph to create purple silk screen used by *Vanity Fair* to accompany the 1984 *Purple Fame* article about the sexual style of Prince and his music. Goldsmith was given credit for the source photograph in the magazine.

Warhol continued to use Goldsmith's photograph to create fifteen additional works in his *Prince Series*. When Warhol died in 1987, the *Prince Series* passed to the Andy Warhol Foundation ("AWF").

Goldsmith photograph, 1981 | *Andy Warhol illustration, Vanity Fair, May 1984*

AWF subsequently transferred the ownership and/or custody of the *Prince Series* to collectors, galleries and the Andy Warhol Museum. AWF retained the copyrights in the works.

When Prince died in 2016, *Conde Nast* asked AWF about reusing the 1984 illustration and learned of the other images in the *Prince Series*. *Conde Nast* selected the *Orange Prince* silk screen and paid AWF a $10,000.00 license fee to use the image on the cover of a magazine commemorating Prince. Warhol cropped, flattened, traced, and colored Goldsmith's original photo to create his silk screen, but did not otherwise alter it. Goldsmith was neither credited nor paid.

Goldsmith saw the magazine and immediately recognized her photograph. She notified AWF of her belief that *Orange Prince* infringed her copyright. Lawsuits, countersuits, and appeals ensued. Through a series of legal twists and stipulations, the matter ended up before the United States Supreme Court on a very limited issue.

The Very Limited Issue

The sole issue decided by the Supreme Court was the narrow question of "whether the first fair use factor, the purpose and character of the use" weighed in favor or against AWF's licensing of *Orange Prince* to *Conde Nast.*

NOT the Issue, NOT the Ruling, NOT decided

The Supreme Court did not opine on whether there was a copyright infringement. It did not analyze whether the second, third and fourth fair use factors as AWF did not challenge the 2nd Circuit's findings that those factors weighed in Goldsmith's favor.

It did not decide or express an opinion on the creation, display, or sale of any other works in Warhol's *Prince Series*. The Court also noted that the first factor might weigh in Warhol's favor if *Orange Prince* was used for teaching purposes or to illustrate an art magazine about Warhol.

The Actual Ruling

The Court ruled that Goldsmith's original use and Warhol's copying use - licensing an image of Prince for use as magazine illustration - shared substantially the same commercial purpose. Therefore, the first fair use factor favored Goldsmith, not Warhol. The Court stated, "Goldsmith's original works, like those of other photographers, are entitled to copyright protection, even against famous artists."

The majority opinion penned by Justice Sotomayor lays out how the reasoning use to reach this result.

The Majority Rules

The Supreme Court did not see Warhol's *Orange Prince* as 'transformative". "Transformativeness", it explained, is a matter of degree. Most copying has some further purpose. Many copies add some new expression, meaning, or message. This is not enough. A copier's use must go beyond the scope of the right to make derivative works (a.k.a. the adaptation right) reserved to the copyright owner.

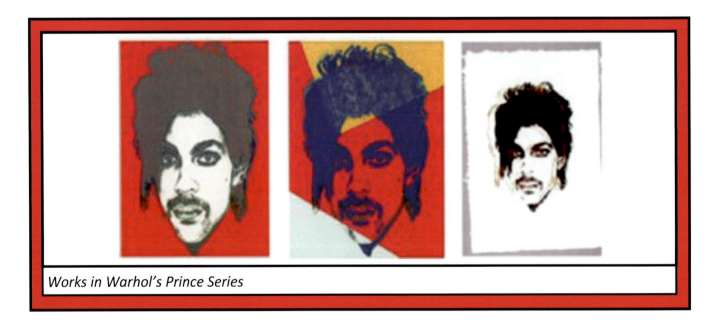

Works in Warhol's Prince Series

In theory, the following points are separate inquiries:

- Whether the original work itself has been transformed? A distinct artistic purpose must reasonably be perceived from the secondary work itself. The subjective intent of the artist is not relevant.
- Whether the copying work has transformative use or purpose? What the user actually does with the work counts.

In practice, as in this case, the questions often overlap. Other first factor inquiries are:

- Whether or not the copying work is used for commercial purposes? A commercial use may or may not weigh against fair use. It is not determinative.
- Whether the use is justified? Justification, like "transformativeness" is a question of degree.

Parody, criticism, and commentary that target the original work clearly serve a different purpose than the original work and are generally fair uses. Uses which share the same or highly similar purposes with the original are generally not.

Soup Cans, for example

The same copying may be fair for one purpose and unfair for another. For example, Warhol's artistic paintings precisely replicating the Campbell's Soup copyrighted logo did not share the same purpose. Warhol's *Soup Can Series* use of Campbell's logo to comment on consumerism was fair. If Warhol had licensed one of those paintings to a different soup company to use as its logo, it would not be fair.

Although, Warhol's *Prince Series* as a whole may comment on the dehumanizing nature of celebrity, this new meaning or message did not make AWF's licensing use of *Orange Prince* "transformative" or fair. That particular use, like a musical arrangement, film or stage adaptation, or a sequel should have been licensed.

Concurring Opinion

The concurring opinion underscores the case's narrow scope: the correct interpretation of "purpose" and "character" of the first factor of the fair use statute.

An inquiry into the purpose and character of a copying work does not focus on the purpose the creator had in mind or the character of the resulting work. The appropriate focus is the specific purpose and character of the challenged use.

In other words, Warhol's intent to comment on celebrity and *Orange Prince*'s new aesthetic did not make the purpose and character of his use different. Rather, the specific purpose of his challenged use -- licensing the image to a magazine – was the same.

In their opinion(s)

Dissenting opinions, like concurring opinions, are *not* binding law. Majority decisions are. Future cases are required to follow majority decisions.

Dissents appeal to "the intelligence of a future day" when a decision in a later case may overturn a majority opinion. Dissents contribute to public debate and sometimes propel legislative changes to the law.

The Dissent

The vigorous dissent declares that the majority neither realized nor cared how much Warhol added. It asks, "If Warhol does not get credit for transformative copying, who will?"

It provides an illustrated history of works building on prior works, ranging from the 16th century reclining nudes of Giorgione and Titian and Manet's 19th century Olympia, to Francis Bacon's 1953 *Study after Velázquez's Portrait of Pope Innocente* X, based on a Velázquez's 1650 work. It proclaims that the majority approach will impede creative progress.

Take away

The dueling opinions demonstrate that legal minds differ vigorously on whether follow-on works are permissible fair uses, or are prohibited derivative uses reserved to the original author.

Clearly, there are indeed very few bright lines in this area of law. An increase in licensing in the grey areas is predicted. It is better to ask permission than apologize later in this arena.

Transformative, For Example

Andrea Blanch, an accomplished professional fashion and portrait photographer, published her photographs in commercial magazines, photography periodicals and collections, and advertisements for widely recognized brands like Revlon, Johnny Walker, and Valentino.

One of Blanch's photographs, *Silk Stockings,* appeared as part of a 6 page feature, *Gilt Trip,* in the August 2000 issue of Allure magazine. *Silk Stockings* depicts a woman's lower legs and feet shot at close range, adorned with bronze nail polish and glittery Gucci sandals, resting on a man's lap in what appears to be a first-class airplane cabin. Blanch composed the shot to "show some sort of erotic sense[;] . . . to get . . . more of a sexuality to the photographs."

Jeff Koons is one of the most prominent, controversial and highly paid artists in the contemporary art field. Koons is known for incorporating objects and images taken from popular media and consumer advertising into his artwork. His work has been shown in major galleries and museums throughout the world.

Niagara was part of Koons' *Easyfun-Ethereal* series, commissioned by the Guggenheim and Deutsche Bank. Koons created the paintings in the series by scanning images culled from advertisements or his own photographs into a computer and superimposing them digitally on pastoral landscapes. The resulting collages were printed and used as templates for his assistants to paint billboard sized canvasses.

The Koons painting was composed of the *Silk Stockings* legs and three other pairs of women's legs dangling prominently over images of confections -- a large chocolate fudge brownie topped with ice cream, a tray of donuts, and a tray of apple danish pastries -- with a grassy field and Niagara Falls in the background.

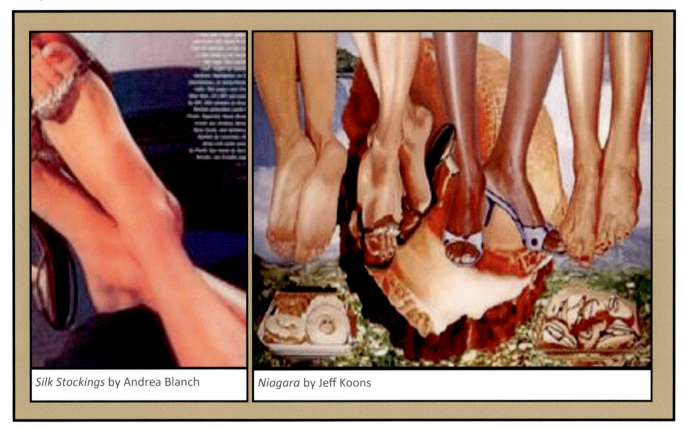

Silk Stockings by Andrea Blanch

Niagara by Jeff Koons

Koons intended the juxtaposition to "comment on the ways in which some of our most basic appetites -- for food, play, and sex – are mediated by popular images." Blanch did not see things that way. When Blanch recognized the legs from her *Silk Stockings* photograph in Jeff Koon's *Niagara* painting, she saw a copyright infringement and filed a lawsuit.

The 2nd Circuit found that Koons's use of a fashion photograph with changes in color and background as part of a massive painting to comment on the social and aesthetic consequences of mass media was clearly transformative. It had a new purpose. *Niagara* altered *Silk Stockings* with new expression, meaning or message.

Although Koons made a substantial profit on *Niagara*, the substantially transformative purpose of his Niagara outweighed the commercial nature of his use.

Blanch's argument that Koons' failure to request permission to use her photograph showed bad faith was rejected. No permission is needed if a use is otherwise fair. Fair use is the right to use copyrighted work without permission or payment in some circumstances. Koons use of Silk Stockings in Niagara was such a circumstance.

The Second Factor

The second factor is:

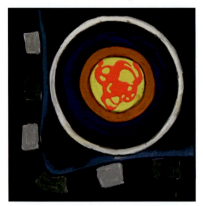

(2) the **nature** of the **copyrighted work.**

Factor 2 by Deborah Reid © 2019

The copyrighted work is the work that was used, fairly or unfairly, to create the later work. Its "nature" has two components:

- how close it is to the core of copyright protection
- whether it was published or unpublished.

Core Strength

The swirling pink inside the yellow represents the core for copyright protection – creative expression. The further from the core the less protection. Facts, ideas, and methods fall outside of the protected zone.

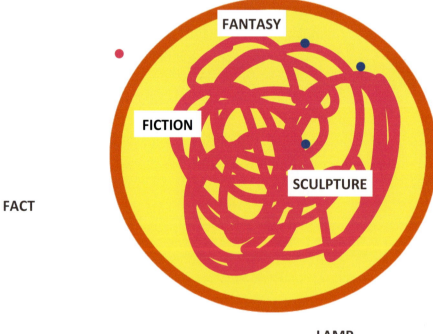

Core Strength by Deborah Reid © 2019

Copyright protection is stronger where the copyrighted material is fiction, not fact. For example, where it is a motion picture rather than a news broadcast. Greater leeway is given for a claim of fair use where the work is factual or informational. Information about current events is not the creation of the writer, it is the history of the day.

Copyright protection is strong where the work serves an artistic rather than a utilitarian purpose. Computer programs almost always serve utilitarian purposes.

Works at the core of copyright protection - lyrics, artistically composed photographs, and fictional works - have been famously used fairly. Roy Orbison's *Oh, Pretty Woman* lyrics were fairly used in 2 Live Crew's parody *Nasty Woman*. Andrea Blanch's glamorous photograph of a woman's legs was fairly included in Jeff Koons' *Niagara* painting. Many of the works copied by Google in the "book-search" project were works of fiction.

(Un) Published?

The second factor weighs against fair use when the copyrighted work is not published. Publication of an author's expression before she has authorized its dissemination seriously infringes the right to decide when and whether it will be made public. This is an infringement of the author's exclusive right of distribution.

Secondary Role

The second factor rarely plays a significant role in the determination of fair use disputes.

The Third Factor

The third factor to be considered is:

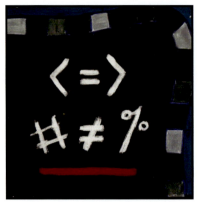

(3) the **amount** and **substantiality** of the portion used in relation to the copyrighted work as a whole.

Factor 3 by Deborah Reid © 2019

The clear implication of this factor is that a finding of fair use is more likely when small amounts, or less important passages, are copied than when the copying is extensive, or encompasses the most important parts of the original.

The obvious reason for this is the relationship between the third and the fourth factors. The larger the amount, or the more important the part of the original that is copied, the greater the likelihood that the secondary work might serve as an effectively competing substitute for the original.

The third statutory factor focuses on how much of the first work was copied. Some courts also look at how much of the second, allegedly infringing work, the copied work comprises.

In both instances, as a general rule:

> Less is more,
>
> but not always.

No Formula – Really

Despite a persistent urban myth, there is no number of words, notes or percentage of change that can be made on Photoshop or software (media) that ensures a use will be fair use. Some of the rumored formulas are based on industry standards, such as newsroom rules for the number of allowable words to be used verbatim from quotes. Others are pulled from the air. None are legally recognized.

The Heart of the Matter

President Gerald Ford granted former President Richard M. Nixon a full pardon after his resignation from office for abuses of power revealed by the investigation into the break-in to the Democratic National Committee's office in the Watergate office complex. There was considerable speculation as to why President Ford issued the pardon. Shortly after leaving office, Gerald Ford contracted with Harper & Row Publishers for the exclusive right to publish his yet to be written memoir. Ford agreed not to publicly discuss previously undisclosed information, such as why he pardoned Nixon.

The publishers licensed the exclusive right to print prepublication excerpts of the memoir to *Time Magazine*. On the eve of *Time*'s pre-publication article, an undisclosed source provided a competitor, *The Nation Magazine*, with a copy of Ford's manuscript. *The Nation*'s editor worked feverishly to produce a short article timed to scoop *Time*'s upcoming article. *Time* cancelled its contract with the publishers and did not remit an agreed upon payment. The publishers sued *The Nation* for copyright infringement.

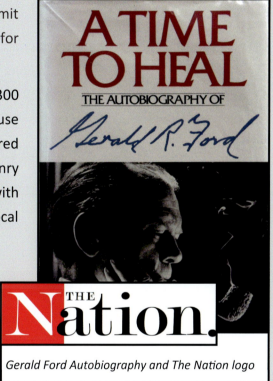

Even though *The Nation* quoted only approximately 300 copyrightable words of the 454 page book, the third fair use factor weighed against it. *The Nation*'s article was structured around verbatim quotes about Ford's conversations with Henry Kissinger and his impressionistic depictions of Nixon, ill with phlebitis after the resignation. The quotes were dramatic focal points of *The Nation*'s article.

These 300 words were "essentially the heart of the book". Quality prevailed over quantity. The substantiality of the material taken outweighed the brevity of the selection. *The Nation*'s use was a copyright infringement not a fair use.

Gerald Ford Autobiography and The Nation logo

For ease of comparison, we note that the text in this section of the page and the following paragraph is 316 words.

The Nation's initial argument that its copying should be given wider latitude than generally afforded by fair use to protect freedom of the press was rejected. The Supreme Court has consistently held that the fair use doctrine, with its latitude for scholarship and commentary, along with the fact/expression dichotomy, embody and protect First Amendment values.

The Whole Thing

Dorling Kindersley ("DK Publishing") published *Grateful Dead: The Illustrated Trip ("Illustrated Trip")* in collaboration with Grateful Dead Productions. The 480-page coffee table book chronicles the cultural history of the Grateful Dead with a collaged timeline combining explanatory text, graphic art, and over 2000 images.

Bill Graham Archives ("BG Archives") owned the copyright to concert posters included as 2" x 3" thumbnails in the timeline without its permission. In response to BG Archive's suit for copyright infringement, DK Publishing successfully argued that even though it used complete copies of each of the concert posters, their use was a fair use.

The courts agreed that DK Publishing's use of the complete images was fair. Even though copying a work in its entirety militates against such a finding, it does not preclude it. In such instances, the inquiry focuses on whether the extent of the copying is necessary to further "the purpose and character of the use".

In this case, DK Publishing's use was meant to commemorate landmark shows in the Grateful Dead's history. "While the fact of these shows could be demonstrated without the use of the thumbnail reproductions of the work, the creative nature of the relevant promotional materials could not be conveyed as effectively without the use of several samples of the work in their entirety. The third factor, therefore, favors defendants."

The 2nd Circuit also noted that although each piece was reproduced in their entirety, they were displayed among hundreds of other images and text, and were only a small part of the *Illustrated History*. The 2" x 3" reproductions did not capture the essence or "heart" of the original full size concert poster.

The Fourth Factor

The fourth factor is:

(4) the **effect of the use** upon the **potential market** for or value of the **copyrighted work**.

Factor 4 by Deborah Reid © 2019

This factor is undoubtedly the single most important element of fair use.

A goal of copyright is to incentivize new creative works by enabling their creators to monetize their work. This goal is thwarted if uses which are mere substitutes are allowed. Potential purchasers could opt for the substitute instead of the original.

The fourth factor and the first factor (the purpose and character of the use) are intertwined. When a use is transformative, it is less likely to disrupt the market for the original.

Pictures, Purposes and Profit

Lawrence Schwartzwald photographed actor Jon Hamm walking down the street holding his girlfriend's hand for the purpose of commercial news reporting "to illustrate what Jon Hamm looks like walking down the street ostensibly without any underwear". Schwartzwald licensed the image to a stock photography agency, the *New York Daily News*, and other third party media outlets.

Oath, Inc., a for profit media company that owns and operates the website www.HuffPost.com., included a modified version of Schwartzwald's photograph in *25 Things You Wish You Hadn't Learned in 2013 and Must Forget in 2014.* The Oath image cropped out Hamm's girlfriend and added 'Image Loading' in a strategically placed text box.

Oath's fair use defense was successful. Oath's use was ruled to be transformative for the same reason; it was not likely have a negative impact on Schwartzwald's market. Oath's image commented on the silliness of the subject while masking the portion of the image that would actually illustrate the actor's appearance sans underwear (ostensibly). The risk was low that any media outlet would purchase Oath's image to illustrate what it did not show.

CMG's fair use defense in an earlier gossip website case tanked. CMG's business model turned on displaying, often without authorization, paparazzi photographs (that it admittedly could not afford to license) to drive traffic to its site and illustrate its celebrity content.

The copyright in some of the photographs CMG used were owned by Barcroft Media and Fame Flynet Inc. Barcroft acquired the copyrights through employment, assignment, and work-for-hire agreements with photographers. CMG's unauthorized use was uncovered by a tracking service that registers copyrights and monitors digital use of images.

Although the collaging and adding text to an image can be transformative, appending "Daily Dump" (the title of CMG's link round up) was not. CMG used the images for the same purpose as Barcroft and Fame Flynet – to document the comings and goings of celebrities.

CMG's use posed a decidedly negative threat to the market for the original. If gossip and entertainment websites could use paparazzi images for free, there would be little or no reason to pay for them.

Go-to-Market

As seen in the paparazzi cases, the effect of the market impact is not limited to harm caused by the particular use, but also if similar widespread uses would adversely impact the market for the original.

Harm to the potential market for derivative works is also considered. The right to make derivative works is one of the rights in the author's exclusive bundle. It is often referred to as the adaptation right. A change in the media, rather than the message or content, is often a defining characteristic of a derivative work. For example, a painting of an image in a photograph.

We go now to Dr. Seuss as an example.

Do Not Pass Go!

Dr. Seuss's last book, *Oh, the Places You'll Go!*, has been a consistent number one best seller during graduation seasons. It is also the basis for several licensed derivative works such as the following books: *Oh, the Things You Can Do that Are Good for You!*; *Oh, the Places I'll Go! By ME, Myself*; *Oh, Baby, the Places You'll Go!*; and *Oh, the Places I've Been! A Journal.*

Oh, the Places You'll Boldly Go! (*Boldly*) is a mash-up. A mash-up is "something created by combining elements from two or more sources" such as "a movie or video having characters or situations from other sources."

Boldly, combined the graphic style and story line of *Oh, the Places You'll Go!* (liberally and without permission) with Captain Kirk and his starship *Enterprise* to tell readers that "life is an adventure but it will be tough." *Boldly*'s creators thought it was a fair use of *Oh, the Places You'll Go!*, but acknowledged that "people in black robes" may disagree. They did, indeed.

The fourth factor (and indeed all the others) weighed against fair use. Widespread production of possible mash-ups like *Oh the Places Yoda'll Go!, Oh the Places You'll Pokemon Go!* could negatively impact the market for licensing *Oh, the Places You'll Go!* derivative works. *Boldly's* release was also targeted for *Oh, the Places You'll Go!*'s peak sales season.

Criticism is Encouraged

Although biting criticism and scathing reviews may suppress demand, they are not copyright infringements or compensable. They are free speech.

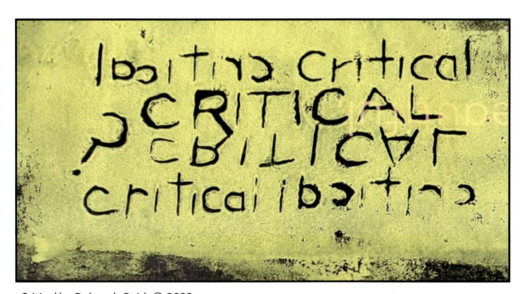

Critical by Deborah Reid © 2022

All Together Now!

Fair use is a holistic, context sensitive inquiry. The four statutory fair use factors are weighed together to answer two interrelated questions:

Interrelated Question by Deborah Reid © 2022

Q1. Does the second work have a different purpose, i.e., is it transformative?

Appropriate Answer: Yes

Q2. Does it act as a substitute and negatively impact the market for the first?

Appropriate Answer: No

If answered appropriately, then fair use is found.

Four More (Stories NOT Factors)

That's Not Fair

Violent Hues Productions, a film festival organizer, use of a cropped version of photographer Brammer's time lapse photo of the Adams Morgan neighborhood in D.C. on its website to illustrate nearby tourist attractions was not a fair use. Its purpose – to depict the neighborhood – was the same as the purpose of Brammer's original photograph.

Brammer v. Violent Hues Productions LLV 922 F.3d 255 (4th Cir 2019)

Despite Koon's assertion that his sculpture at top, was a satirical critique of materialism, his use of the photograph below, was not fair.

Change in media is a classic derivative use, a right reserved to authors.

Rogers v. Koons, 467 F.3d 244 (2d Cir. 2006)

Fair Enough

	Art gallery's use of photographs and plans of Cady Noland's *Log Cabin Façade* to market the work for resale was a fair use. The U.S. Copyright Office subsequently rejected Noland's application to register the work as a sculpture on ground that it lacked originality. *Noland v. Janssen,* 2020 U.S. Dist. LEXIS 95454 (S.D.N.Y. 2020).
A news reports about a viral video livestreaming a baby's birth including brief excerpts and a screen shot were fair use. *Konangataa v. Am. Broadcasting Companies, Inc.,* 2017 U.S. Dist. LEXIS 95812 (S.D.N.Y. June 21, 2017).	

Fair Well.

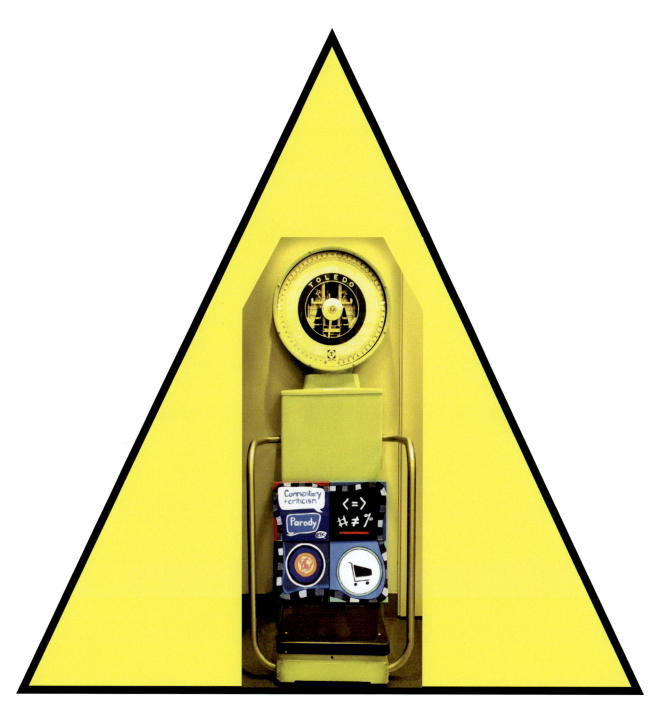

CAVEAT CREATOR ♦ ARTIST BEWARE

The Legal Care and Protection of Copyright

Notices, Registration, Litigation and Other Tools

THE LEGAL CARE AND PROTECTION OF COPYRIGHT

Giving Your Notice
The Elements of Notice ✦ Where to Put It

Registration
Starting With Why ✦ For Lawsuits, Registration Means Registration, Not Application
Registration DIY ✦ The Application ✦ The Application: Author(s) ✦ Creation and Publication
Safe Harbors and Help ✦ $ x $ x $ x $ = Money + Multiples
Deposit Copies Are Not Mandatory Deposits

Infringement
What is Copyright Infringement? ✦ What Do You Have to Prove? ✦ You Have to Own It
And Then, and Then… ✦ Pink Coats, Piggy Backs

Cease and Desist!

Lawsuits
Glossary of Infringement Remedies ✦ Time Matters
A Few Final Words About Lawsuits

The CASE Act
There Are Limitations ✦ It's All Volunteer ✦ Benefits of CCB Proceedings

The Digital Millennium Copyright Act
Safe Harbors ✦ A Step by Step Guide to the System ✦ Anti-Circumvention
There Are (Evolving) Exemptions ✦ There Are Serious Consequences

Giving Your Notice

You are automatically the owner of the copyright in original works you create. Although copyright notices have not been required since 1989, it is still a good idea to use them.

Copyright notices let people know that they need the copyright owner's approval to use the work. Many people respect this limitation. Some do not.

The Elements of Notice

A copyright notice has three elements:

© the word copyright, its abbreviation or symbol, ©

© the year of first publication of the work*

© the name of the copyright owner

Some examples:

Mary Atwood, Copyright, 2022

M. Atwood, copr. 2022

Mary Atwood© 2022

It is alright to add "All rights reserved" to the mix, but not to use it as a stand-alone:

Mary Atwood, © All rights reserved, 2022	Mary Atwood, All rights reserved, 2022
YES	NO

Where to Put It

For paintings, prints, photographs and other two-dimensional copies, you can put the copyright notice on the front or the back of the piece, the mounting, matting, framing or other material to which the work is affixed.

For sculpture and other three-dimensional works, you can put the copyright notice on any visible part of the work, a mounting, base or other material in which it is permanently housed.

Notices should be durably attached in ways that will withstand normal use.

Registration

Starting with Why

Federal copyright protection starts from the work's creation. An author gains exclusive rights in her work immediately upon the work's creation, including rights of reproduction, distribution, and display.

The existence of an author's rights is not dependent on registration of the copyright. An author's ability to sue for infringement is.

A work must be registered with the Copyright Office before a lawsuit for its infringement can be filed in federal court. Registration is also prerequisite for certain types of relief to be granted.

Mailing a copy of the work to yourself and keeping the sealed postmarked envelope is not a viable alternative to registration. It is a mistaken urban myth.

For Lawsuits, Registration Means Registration, Not Application

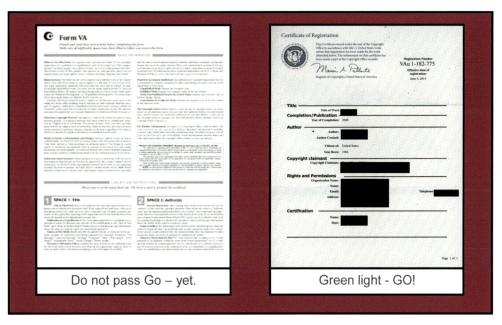

Filing an application for registration does not mean that the work is registered. Registration occurs after the Copyright Office reviews and actually registers the copyright. The time between filing an application and registration of a copyright typically takes several months.

A small claims proceeding with the newly formed Copyright Claims Board can be filed along with an application for registration. However, a determination will not be made until a registration certificate is actually filed.

Registration DIY

The U.S. Copyright Office strongly encourages use of its online system to register a copyright. The online system has lower filing fees; faster processing and status tracking, payment by credit card, debit card, or electronic check; and optional deposit upload. Paper applications are slower, more expensive and discouraged.

To get started with the online system, go to the Electronic Copyright Office (eCO) @ https://eservice.eco.loc.gov/siebel/app/eservice/enu?SWECmd=Start.

First set up an account with your user ID, password and contact information. You are now ready to complete applications, save drafts and track your submissions.

Be sure you are on the official site with the ". gov" address. There are a lot of commercial websites dressed up to look like official sites that charge additional fees to process applications.

Copyright registration has three parts

- a completed application
- filing fee payment
- and a deposit copy of the work

Each step must be completed before moving to the next.

The Application

Copyright applications establish the basic facts of copyright claims including the type of work, its title, the author and/or copyright owner, and their contact information.

All of the information on the application is available to the public online. The deposit copy also becomes part of the public record.

The basic registration forms include:

Literary Form TX

Visual Form VA

Single Serials Form SE

Performing Arts PA Sound

Recording Forms SR

Standard

Published Photographs

Unpublished Photographs

A Group of Unpublished Works

Form VA, US Copyright Office

As this tome is a guide for visual artists, we will use Visual Form VA as an example. Form VA is used to register single works of visual art. Visual art includes two and three-dimensional works of fine, graphic, and applied art, watercolor and oil paintings, logo, illustrations, computer graphics photographs, prints, art reproductions, toys, dolls, scale models, sculptural designs applied to useful articles, maps, globes, charts, technical drawings, diagrams and models and more. Architectural works are not included.

Form VA contains basic information on copyright, how and when to use the form, and line-by-line Instructions for each of eight spaces to be filled in to complete the application.

The basic information of a visual art copyright claim such as the type of work, its title, the author and claimant, and their contact information must be provided.

Most of the instructions and information sought are straightforward. Some sections ask for legal conclusions such as who the author is, and if and when the work was published.

The Application: Author(s)

SPACE 2 asks WAS THIS CONTRIBUTION TO THE WORK A "WORK MADE FOR HIRE"?

A work made for hire is a work that (1) was made within the scope of employment; or (2) as a specially commissioned contribution to a collective work, part of a motion picture or audio visual work, translation, supplementary work, compilation, instructional text, test, answer material for a test, or an atlas.

If the work is one of these, it is a work made for hire whose author is the employer or the person for whom the work was prepared. Works made for hire are covered in the Ownership of Copyright section. Review that information and use the 7 Questions chart to figure out whether a work is a work made for hire.

The Copyright Office now also requires that AI use must be disclosed, detailed, and disclaimed on applications for copyright registration. Works that contain sufficient human input are eligible for registration.

Creation and Publication

SPACE 3 asks you to provide the year of creation and the date and nation of first publication. Creation and publication are different. A work is created when it is fixed for the first time. i.e., it is fixed when you actually sculpt the sculpture, not when you first think about the sculpture you want to create. (See, Part 2, Section, Fixation.)

The question of publication is a little more nuanced. The terms publication and publishing have a long and twisty history in copyright law. Basically, publication means distributing the work to the public OR offering to distribute the work to the public.

Prior to 1989, publishing a work without a proper copyright notice could result in the work becoming ineligible for copyright protection and a part of the public domain. Fortunately, this is no longer the case.

Publication remains significant for a number of reasons. For example, the year of publication may determine the length of copyright protection for works made for hire, anonymous or pseudonymous works. The applicability of some limitations and exceptions to copyright law depend on whether a work is published or unpublished. Deposit requirements for unpublished and published works also differ.

Safe Harbors and Help

Making an inadvertent mistake on an application will not later invalidate a registration certificate. Knowingly providing inaccurate factual information or legal conclusions will.

The Copyright Act provides a safe harbor for certificates with inaccurate information that would have caused the application to be rejected provided the applicant did not know the information was inaccurate. The safe harbor exists to make it easier for painters, poets, designers, and other non-lawyers to obtain valid copyright registrations.

The Copyright Office staff is knowledgeable, helpful and courteous. Take advantage of their expertise and ask for their help.

The Copyright Office cannot provide legal advice. If you have a legal question, ask a lawyer. If you need legal assistance, get an attorney.

$ x $ x $ x $ = Money + Multiples

Single author, same claimant, one work, not for hire	$45.00*
Published or unpublished photographs - online only	$55.00
All other standard applications online	$65.00
Group of unpublished works – online only	$85.00
Registrations on paper	$125.00
Group of updates for photographic database	$250.00
Group of updates for nonphotographic database – paper only	$500.00
	$$$$$$$$$$$$$

* Fees subject to change

If you are a prolific non-photographer, it can add up.

One option to cut filing costs is to register a group of unpublished works online. Up to ten unpublished works can be registered at a time for a single fee.

Unpublished means that you have not distributed the work or copies of it to the public by sale or other transfer of ownership or offered to distribute the work to a group for purposes of further distribution.

This option is available if, and only if:

- All of the works are unpublished
- All works are created by the same author or joint authors
- All of the authors are named as copyright claimants
- The contribution of each author to each work must be the same, i.e. unpublished illustrations
- Each work must have a title
- Each work has to be in the same class, i.e. VA (visual art)
- Filed online
- Digital copies are deposited

Photographers can register a group of up to 750 published photographs, subject to similar limitations if all of the photographs were published in the same year. Photographers also have the option to register up to 750 unpublished photographs as a group.

Other options for registration of more than one work at a time include registration of serials, newspapers, newsletters, contributions to periodicals, database updates and revision, questions, answers and other items prepared for secure tests, and groups of works first published together as a single integrated unit.

 *You will get a lot of scam solicitations when you file to register your copyright.*

Deposit Copies Are Not Mandatory Deposits

There are "deposit copies" and "mandatory copies". They satisfy different requirements.

Deposit copies are what you submit with your application for registration. For visual arts and three-dimensional works such as sculpture and jewelry, you do not send the actual item. You send "identifying material" such as photographs, illustrations or drawings that clearly identifies the work being registered.

You can contact the Copyright Office helpline for questions regarding the deposit requirement for a particular work.

Copyright owners have been required to submit two copies of published works to the Library of Congress since the early 1800s. This requirement is not connected to registration and applies to unregistered works as well. The purpose is to build the Library's collection.

If you get a Notice of Mandatory Deposit of Copies from the Copyright Office, be flattered and submit the copies. You will be in the Library of Congress collection. Not all published authors are.

For works published in the United States, the 1976 Copyright Act contains a provision under which a single deposit can be made to satisfy both the deposit requirements for the Library and the registration requirements. In order to have this dual effect, the copies or phonorecords must be accompanied by the prescribed application form and filing fee.

Library of Congress by Deborah Reid © 2016

Infringement

What is Copyright Infringement?

Remember the bundle of exclusive rights? Here is an annotated bouquet for a refresher.

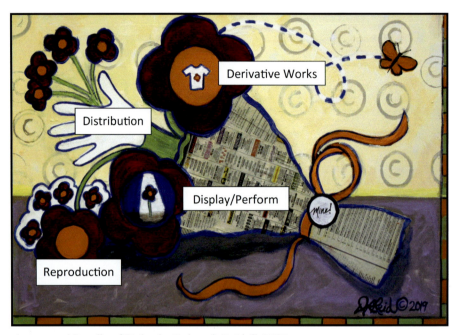

Annotated Bundle of Rights by Deborah Reid © 2022

Whenever anyone exercises one of your exclusive rights without your permission, it is a copyright infringement. Whenever you exercise someone else's exclusive rights without their permission, it is copyright infringement.

The quick click of a key or routine downloads can be infringements. It doesn't matter if you knew it was an infringement or even that you intended to flatter the copyright owner by gratuitously displaying their work.

Actions, including seemingly innocuous or laudable actions, count. Intent is irrelevant.

What Do You Have to Prove?

There are two core elements of a claim for copyright infringement. To win an infringement claim, you must prove both:

1. You are the copyright owner

+

2. Someone else used your work or the original copyrightable components of it to create

<u>a SUBSTANTIALLY SIMILAR WORK without your authorization</u>

= COPYRIGHT INFRINGEMENT

You Have to Own It

First things first. You must first prove that you own the copyright in an original work that has been fixed in a tangible medium.

A certificate of copyright registration issued by the Copyright Office initially satisfies this requirement. Registration is also required before an infringement lawsuit can begin in federal court or a CASE small claims case can be decided.

And Then, and Then . . .

Mary on Mary by Deborah Reid © 2022

Once you establish copyright ownership, you then have to prove that an exclusive right was exercised without your authorization. This can be straightforward. For example, if someone prints an exact copy of your very stylized, Photoshop enhanced photo on a t-shirt without your permission, it is an infringement of your exclusive right to make derivative works.

More often, the analysis is considerably more complex. As only the original copyrightable parts of your work are protected, other components have to be thrown out. To figure out what parts are protected and what parts are not, you have to figure out what parts are in the public domain and what parts are not. Nuanced questions of copyrightability, like where unprotectible ideas end and protectible expressions start, have to be answered.

Once your work is pared down to its protectible elements, you compare it to the unauthorized work to decide whether the works are substantially similar. This determination, like the idea/expression divide, is very complex. Different circuits have different tests for substantial similarity. The tests are similar.

Here is a story from the 1st Circuit that sorts things and shows how a legal analysis of copyright infringement works

Pink Coats, Piggy Backs

| Harney photograph | Sony photograph |

Donald A. Harney, a freelance photographer, snapped a picture of young blonde girl, Reigh "Snooks" Rockefeller, in a pink coat riding on her father's shoulders leaving a Palm Sunday service. His photograph was published on the front page of the Beacon Hill Times.

The photo became a media sensation a year later when the father abducted his daughter during a custodial visit. The photo played a prominent role in the daughter's safe return and her father's arrest.

Harney did not object to the FBI's use of the photo in a "WANTED" poster. He licensed the photograph to various media outlets including Vanity Fair.

Harney did object to Sony Pictures' use of its own photograph of a young blonde girl in a pink coat riding piggy back in its docudrama *Who Is Clark Rockefeller?* Clark Rockefeller was one of many identities assumed by Christian Karl Gerhartsreiter, Reigh's father, who is currently serving time for murder.

To determine whether Sony's picture was a copyright infringement, the court dissected and compared the images to determine if use of original expressive elements of Harney's work resulted in a substantially similar work.

A rule refresher and a chart of the court's dissection, comparison and analysis follow.

Facts, like ideas, are not protected by copyright. They are not copyrightable.

Protectible original expressive elements of photographs include posing the subjects, lighting, angle, timing, focus and other variants. These elements are copyrightable.

Element	CAN	NOT	WHY
The pink coat		X	Harney did not style the subjects. He came across a little girl wearing a pink coat. It was real. It was a fact.
The piggy back pose		X	Same analysis as the pink coat above.
The background	Yes, but		Framing the pair against backdrop of a church with bright blue sky and prominent shadows was copyrightable, but it was not copied.
Positioning the pair in middle of frame looking straight into camera at close distance	Yes		This involved aesthetic judgments that contributed to the photo's impact.

The court found that Sony's photograph was not an infringement of Harney's photograph. The two photographs are notably different in lighting and coloring. The impression of similarity was due largely to the piggyback pose which was not copyrightable. The placement of the subjects in the center of the frame was only minimally original and was not enough to support a finding of substantial similarity required for infringement.

Cease and Desist!

A cease and desist letter is one of the simplest tools to use to protect your copyright. It basically says, "Stop infringing my copyright, or else".

"Or else" includes take down notices, injunctions and lawsuits. If you are not prepared to follow through on the "or else", be prepared to have your bluff called.

Cease and desist letters should include:

- A description of your copyrighted work.
- A copy of the copyright registration certificate, if you have one.
- A statement of how they are infringing your work.
- A demand that the infringement stop within a specific time.
- A statement of what you will do if the infringement does not stop.
- A demand for written agreement that the infringement will stop.
- A demand for an accounting of their profits and location of any infringing products.

Cease and desist letters sent by lawyers often carry more weight. Cease and desist letters have pros and cons. Here are some:

Pros	Cons
Cheap	You reveal your legal strategy
May lead to a resolution	It may not lead to a resolution
You may obtain helpful information about the infringer's opinion and use of your work	An unlikely possibility: The infringer could file a lawsuit against you asking for a ruling that they are not infringing
ISPs often encourage use prior to take downs	

Lawsuits

Copyright infringement lawsuits must be filed in federal courts. A few introductory words about lawsuits:

> Grueling. Stressful. Complicated. Expensive.
>
> Don't do it yourself. Hire a qualified attorney.

If you are able to prove that your copyright was infringed, you may be entitled to some, but not all, of the remedies listed and then defined below:

List of Infringement Remedies

Injunction

+/OR

$ Copyright Owner's Actual Damages $

+

$ Infringer's Profits $

OR

$ Statutory Damages $

+

$ Attorney's Fees and Costs $

+/OR

Impoundment + Destruction

If you infringe someone else's copyright, they may be able to get all or some of the above, from you.

Glossary of Infringement Remedies

Injunctions: An injunction is an order to stop doing something or to do something. The first type of injunction – STOP! – is the most common.

In copyright actions, federal courts will generally issue injunctions after infringement and liability have been established if there is a likely threat of future violations.

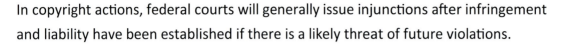

Copyright Owner's Actual Damages: Damages are the amount of money that a person who is harmed is entitled to get from the person who caused the harm. A copyright owner is entitled to recover the actual damages suffered as a result of an infringement. This means that the copyright owner is entitled to be paid the income it actually lost or the fair market value of a license for the infringer's use.

AND

Infringer's Profits: A copyright owner is entitled to recover the infringer's profit from the infringement, if not taken into account in computing actual damages.

Actual damages and infringer's profits are often hard to prove. A myriad of factors unrelated to the infringement, like supply chain glitches, also impact income and profit. Statutory damages are different.

OR

Statutory Damages: Statutory damages are the most common kind of damages in infringement cases. If your copyright was registered before the infringement occurred, or within three months of publication of your work, you can opt to get statutory damages. If not, you cannot get statutory damages.

Statutory damage awards typically range between $750.00 to $30,000.00 for each work infringed by a particular defendant. Statutory damages may be increased to $150,000.00 per infringement if the infringement was willful.

For example, if one person infringed your same work twenty times, you are only entitled to one award of statutory damages. If your work was infringed by two different people, you are entitled to two awards of statutory damages, one from each infringer.

Attorney's Fees and Costs: A court may order the losing party to pay the winning party's attorney's fees and court costs such as filing fees. It may not. This is discretionary.

Impoundment and Destruction: The Copyright Act provides for impoundment of infringing copies while a copyright lawsuit is pending. Infringing copies can be destroyed at the lawsuit's conclusion. The courts can also order that the means to make more infringing copies like film negatives or molds be destroyed. Although it is not done routinely, it is a possibility.

Time Matters

A lawsuit for copyright infringement must be filed within three years of when the infringement occurred. Any lawsuits filed more than three years after the infringement can be barred by the statute of limitations.

A Few Final Words About Lawsuits

CAVEAT CREATOR ♦ ARTIST BEWARE

Expensive. Costly. Expensive.

Not a DIY project.

The average cost of litigation for copyright infringement cases through appeal was up to $397,000.00 in 2019. It will likely continue to increase.

The CASE Act

On an individual level, the prohibitive cost of federal infringement litigation undermines an author's incentive to create and share new work. Played out collectively, it thwarts copyright's purpose of advancing public knowledge by depriving society of the benefits of new expressive works.

The Copyright Alternative in Small-Claims Enforcement Act of 2019 ("CASE Act") was enacted to provide a more affordable venue. The CASE Act established a three judge tribunal in the U.S. Copyright Office to handle smaller claims. Here is what the Copyright Claims Board ("CCB") can do for you.

The maximum amount the Copyright Claims Board can award

There are Limitations

The CCB can award statutory damages of $15,000.00 per work infringed. It can also award actual damages. The maximum total damages the CCB can award in a case is $30,000.00.

Federal courts can award statutory damages of $150,000.00 per work infringed. There is no limit on the amount of total damages a federal court can award in an infringement case.

The CCB cannot order anyone to stop infringing activity. Federal courts can.

It's All Volunteer

The CCB is a voluntary alternative to litigation in federal court.

No one can be compelled to take part in a CCB proceeding due to constitutional constraints. This means you can choose to bring your claim in federal court instead.

It also means if you are named as a respondent in a CCB proceeding you can opt out in a timely fashion.

Benefits of CCB Proceedings

- *DIY Resolutions:* The simpler, streamlined procedures of the CCB are designed to be DIY. Attorneys are completely optional. Law students supervised by licensed attorneys are allowed to represent you.

- *Eliminates costly travel:* You do not have to go to the CCB in person. Unlike proceedings in federal courts, CCB proceedings are designed to be handled entirely by written submissions, Internet applications, and other telecommunication facilities.

- *Registration relief:* You can start (although not finish) a CCB claim once you have filed your application to register your copyright with the U.S. Copyright Office. In federal courts, you cannot file a lawsuit until the registration process is complete. This can take several months.

- *Guidance:* The CCB will make Copyright Claims Attorneys, CCB Handbook, and website available for guidance throughout the process.

The Digital Millennium Copyright Act

In 1998, the Digital Millennium Copyright Act (DMCA) updated U.S. copyright law to address online copyright infringement by adding:

- Safe Harbors and the Notice-and-Takedown System
- Anti-Circumvention Prohibitions
- Copyright Management Information Protection

Safe Harbors

Sunset Harbor by Mary Atwood © 2022

The DMCA provides website operators, search engines, web hosts and online service providers like Facebook, Google, eBay, and YouTube with "safe harbors".

A safe harbor is a legal provision that eliminates liability if certain conditions are met. It provides protection for good-faith actors who may technically violate a law due to reasons beyond their reasonable control.

In exchange for having a Notice-and-Takedown System in place, online companies are shielded from liability for monetary damages for copyright infringement claims due to user generated content. They still have to obey injunctions.

The DMCA, like all copyright law, is territorial. The DMCA only applies to online service providers (a.k.a. Internet service providers or ISPs) located or doing enough business in the U.S., to be within the reach of federal court jurisdiction. That said, many overseas ISPs have voluntarily implemented notice-and-take down procedures.

The notice-and-takedown system is an efficient and cost-effective way to deal with online copyright infringement. If you find your work is being copied, displayed, distributed, or otherwise used online without your permission consider submitting a notice to the ISP of the site where the infringing work is located.

A Step by Step Guide to the System

Step 1 The Takedown Notice

To get infringing work removed from an online site, you send a takedown notice to the ISP. Takedown notices should include the following information:

Many online service providers, like Facebook, Instagram, YouTube and Redbubble have their own online forms. The forms and instructions are often located on the help, customer support, or rules pages of the service provider's website. If they have one, use it.

Blue Door Steps by Mary Atwood © 2023

DMCA Takedown Notice

Your contact information.

A description of the copyrighted material that is being infringed. If you have a copyright registration number, include it here. It is not required but it is persuasive.

Location of the infringing work on the service provider's site.

A statement that that you have a good faith belief that the use of your work was not authorized.

Verification under penalty of perjury that the information in the notice is accurate and that you own the copyrighted material or are acting on behalf of the owner.

The physical or electronic signature of the copyright owner or authorized agent.

Step 2 The ISP takes it down

When the ISP receives a takedown notice, it must "expeditiously" remove or disable access to the material. If it does not, it may lose its safe harbor protection and become liable for copyright infringement.

The ISP must also notify the content poster of the removal and provide an opportunity for a counter notice.

Step 3 Counter-notices

A counter-notice essentially says "The takedown notice is wrong. Put it back up AND . . . . "

Counter-notices should include:

DMCA Counter-Notice

The content

The poster's contact information

A description of the copyrighted material that was removed or disabled.

Location of the infringing work on the service provider's site before removal.

A statement that that you have a good faith belief that the removal was a result of a mistake or misidentification.

Verification under penalty of perjury that the information in the notice is accurate and that you own the copyrighted material or are acting on behalf of the owner.

The physical or electronic signature of the content poster.

AND

Content poster's consent to U.S. jurisdiction and to service of process by mail, or even email.

The last item can be a game changer. It can extend the jurisdiction of U.S. courts to players that would have otherwise been beyond reach.

Step 4 Ten Day Window

In many instances counter-notices are not submitted and the content stays down. If a valid counter-notice is submitted, the copyright holder has 10 days to file a lawsuit in federal court and tell the ISP about it. If not the content goes back up.

Repeat Offenders

In addition to providing notice-and takedown procedures, ISPs must have and enforce repeat offender policies to qualify for safe harbor protection. Many repeat offender policies terminate users who are repeat infringers. Don't be a repeat infringer.

Anti-Circumvention

The Anti-Circumvention provisions of the DMCA were enacted to comply with WIPO Copyright Treaty requirements. These provisions make it illegal to:

descramble a scrambled work,

decrypt an encrypted work, or

otherwise avoid, bypass, remove,

or deactivate technological barriers

put in place by the copyright owner to prevent unauthorized use of digital media.

It is also illegal to remove or alter copyright management information such as copyright notices and terms of use. Providing false copyright management information is also prohibited. 17 USC 1202.

For example, removal of watermarks from photographs is prohibited. So is bypassing Digital Rights Management (DRM) in E-books, films, and games. The distribution of tools or devices that allow others to circumvent tech barriers is also prohibited.

The act of circumventing copy control mechanisms is not illegal. This act was intentionally omitted to preserve fair use rights. Other exceptions continue to evolve.

There are (Evolving) Exemptions

Library browsing, law enforcement and intelligence activities, encryption research by a person who has a lawful right to use a copy of a computer program, are examples of permanent exemptions. There are others.

Every three years, the Library of Congress determines if there should be additional exemptions. The current exemption list is in Code of Federal Regulations.

There are Serious Consequences

On the civil side, violators may be required to pay actual damages, their profits, costs, and attorney's fees. Circumvention devices can be confiscated. Injunctions can be issued.

Violators also face criminal liability. Fines of up to $500,000.00 or five years in prison can be imposed for willful violations for commercial advantage or private financial gain for the first offense. Subsequent offenses are punishable by fines of up to $1,000,000.00 or 10 years in prison.

Make Art.

Share Your Vision.

Enrich Society.

Protect Your Copyrights.

Respect the Rights of Others.

Fair Well.

The End by Deborah Reid and Mary Atwood © 2022

End Notes

Introductory Materials

The Purpose of Copyright

"The primary purpose" *United States v Paramount Pictures, Inc*. 334 U.S. 131 (1948)

"The public is the intended beneficiary" *Fox Film v. Doyal* 286 U.S. 123 (1931)

Applicable Law

Copyright law is dynamic" *Mazer v. Stein,* 347 U.S. 201 (1954)

Copyright Law is Territorial

"Copyright law is "territorial" " *Update Art, Inc. v. Modiin Publishing, Ltd.,* 843 F.2d 67 (2d Cir. 1988)

Copyright and the Constitution

"Copyright law in the United States starts" *Kelley v. Chi. Park. Dist.,* 635 F.3d 290 (7th Cir. 2011)

First AmendmentISH

"Oddly, the First Amendment" *Eldred v. Ashcroft,* 537 U.S. 186 (2003)

Federal Statutes and Treaties

"The U.S. is also party to several international treaties" *Berne Convention for the Protection of Literary and Artistic Works*, as revised. *World International Property Organization (WIPO) Copyright Treaty*

Federal Courts and Cases

"The copyright statutes and treaty provisions " *Topolos v. Caldeway,* 698 F.2d 991 (9th Cir. 1983)

"The 2nd Circuit" Kenneth A. Plevan, *The Second Circuit and the Development of Intellectual Property Law: The First 125 Years,* 85 Fordham L. Rev. 143 (2016)

"The 9th Circuit" William K. Ford, *Judging Experience in Copyright Law,* 14 J.Intell. Prop. L. 1, 41 (2006)

The Law is Identical on the Internet

"Copyright laws apply to online materials" *Digital Millenium Copyright Act,* 17 U.S.C. §1202, et seq.

The Subject Matter of Copyright

A Little History

"In 1440, Johann Gutenberg" https://en.wikipedia.org/wiki/Printing_press

"By the year 1500" https://www.loc.gov/item/myloc8/

"In 1710" Statute of Anne, 1710, 8 Ann., c. 19 (Eng)

"Basically, it means" https://fairuse.stanford.edu/overview/public-domain/welcome/

The Threshold Requirements

"Creative expression is at the core" *Campbell v. Acuff-Rose Music Inc.,* 510 U.S. 569 (1994)

"A work must first satisfy" 17 U.S.C. §102

" "Author" has been defined by the Supreme Court" *Burrows-Giles Lithographic Co. v. Sarony,* 114 U.S. 53 (1884)

"The originality requirement" 17 U.S.C. §102

"Writings" *Goldstein v. California,* 412 U.S. 546 (1973)

"The work must also fall" 17 U.S.C. §102

That's Original

"Originality is the *sine qua non*" *Feist Publications, Inc. v. Rural Tel. Serv. Co., Inc.,* 499 U.S. 340 (1991)

On Photography

"In the 19th century, photography" https://daily.jstor.org/when-photography-was-not-art/

"In 1884, a young Oscar Wilde" *Burrows-Giles Lithographic Co. v. Sarony,* 114 U.S. 53 (1884)

"In 2005, dentist Mitchell A. Pohl" *Pohl v. MH SUB I LLC Offcite,* 2019 U.S. App. LEXIS 13132 (11th Cir. 2019)

Sparks and Bars

"Some creative spark" *Feist Publications Inc. v. Rural Telephone Service Co. Inc.,* 499 U.S. 340 (1991)

"Fortunately for artists" *Bridgeman Art Library v. Corel Corp.,* 36 F.Supp. 2d 191 (S.D.N.Y. 1999); *Schrock v. Learning Curve International Inc.,* 586 F.3d 513 (7th Cir. 2009); Mary Campbell Wojcik, *Bridgeman, Image Licensors and the Public Domain,* 30 Hastings Comm. & Ent. L.J. 257 (2008)

Fix It

"The Copyright Clause", Art. 1, Sec. 8, U.S. Constitution

""Fixed" means" 17 U.S.C. §101.

"A single work can have multiple fixations" *Kelley v. Chicago Park District,* 635 F.3d 290 (7th Cir 2011)

"The fixation requirement for choreography" https://www.copyright.gov/circs/circ52.pdf

Fix Your Makeup

"Sammy Mourabit was the makeup artist" *Mourabit v. Klein,* 393 F. Supp. 3d 353 (S.D.N.Y. 2019)

The Ephemeral Nature of Nature

"Chapman Kelley was a nationally recognized artist" *Kelley V. Chicago Park District,* 635 F.3d 290 (7th Cir 2011)

A Wet Napkin in the Automat

"In 1975, Tom Wolfe" *The Painted Word,* Farrar, Strauss & Giraux, © 1975

Fixation is Not Universal

"While the fixation requirement" White, Elizabeth (2013) *The Berne Convention's Flexible Fixation Requirement: A Problematic Provision for User-Generated Content,* Chicago Journal of International Law: Vol.

13: No. 2, Article 18 (Available at: https://chicagounbound.uchicago.edu/cjil/vol13/iss2/18)

What You CAN Copyright

"Copyright originated and continues to evolve" Orit Fisschman-Afori, *The Evolution of Copyright Law and Inductive Speculations as to Its Future,* Journal of Intellectual Property Law, Spring 2012 (Available at www.digitalcommons.law.uga.edu/cgi/viewcontent.cgi?referer=&httpsredir=1&article=1067&context=jipl)

"The types of work' 17 U.S.C. §102

The Copyrightability of Commercial Works: The Bleistein Principle

"When asked in 1903," *Bleistein v. Donaldson Lithographing Co.,* 188 U.S. 239 (1903)

"The judicial refusal to act" *Alfred Bell v. Catalda,* 191 F.2d 99 (2d Circ. 1951)

"This doctrine of avoidance" *Smith v. Goguen,* 415 U.S. 566 (1974); *Cohen v. California,* 403 U.S. 15 (1971)

What You Can NOT Copyright: Other Intellectual Property

"Intellectual property law is a loose group" https://www.law.cornell.edu/wex/intellectual_property

"The rights of publicity and privacy" *https://www.law.cornell.edu/wex/publicity*

"Copyright is the form that protects original artistic expression" *Campbell v. Acuff-Rose Music, Inc.,* 510 U.S. 569 (1994)

Trademarks: Titles, Mottos, Slogans, Logos, Symbols, Packaging and Cartoon Characters

"Trademark law provides protection" https://www.law.cornell.edu/wex/trademark#:~:text=Definition,%C2%A7%201127

"Trademark law can also provide protection" https://scholarship.shu.edu/cgi

"If trademark is in continuous, use can be extended indefinitely" 15 U.S.C. §1058,105 *Kohler Co. v. Moen, Inc.*, 12 F.3d 632 (7th Cir. 1993)

"Trademarks do not provide universal monopolies" https://www.uspto.gov/trademarks/basics/scope-protection

"Trade dress is a term of art" https://www.law.cornell.edu/wex/trade_dress

Patents: Methods, Inventions, Procedures, Systems, Discoveries and Some Useful Articles

"Patent law protects" https://www.law.cornell.edu/wex/patent

"Design patents" https://www.uspto.gov/ip-policy/patent-policy/industrial-designs

Trade Secrets

"Trade secret law can provide" https://www.law.cornell.edu/wex/trade_secret

"It is still a secret" https://www.coca-colacompany.com/company/history/coca-cola-formula-is-at-the-world-of-coca-cola

THE IDEA/EXPRESSION DIVIDE

The Law of Ideas

"Copyrights do not protect ideas" 17 U.S.C. §102(b)

"Only the expression of the idea" *Baker v. Selden,* 101 U.S. 99 (1879); *Mazer v. Stein,* 347 U.S. 201 (1954)

"Ideas are as free as the air" *Desny v. Wilder,* 46 Cal. 2d 715 (1956)

"Every idea, theory, and fact" *Golan v. Holder,* 565 U.S. 302 (2012)

"This is the idea/expression divide" *Golan v. Holder,* 565 U.S. 302 (2012)

"Where to draw the line " *Nichols v. Universal Pictures Corp.,* 119 F.2d 45 (2d Cir. 1930)

The Starting Line(s)

"The origin story for the idea/expression divide" *Baker v. Selden,* 101 U.S. 99 (1879)

Some Lines are Drawn

"The Supreme Court compared the ruled lines" *Baker v. Selden,* 101 U.S. 99 (1879)

Perspective is Given (or Taken)

"The Court explained" *Baker v. Selden,* 101 U.S. 99 (1879)

Genius is Recognized

"The Supreme Court went on to say" *Baker v. Selden,* 101 U.S. 99 (1879)

Don't Jump

Kaplan v. Stock Market Photo Agency, 133 F. Supp. 2d 317 (S.D.N.Y. 2001)

Watch the Cat + Mouse

Direct Marketing of Va. v. E. Mishan & Sons, Inc., 753 F. Supp 100 (S.D.N.Y. 1990)

Manhattan Mohawk

Kerr v. New Yorker Magazine, 63 F. Supp. 2d 320 (S.D.N.Y. 1999)

The Same Old Story

"Scènes à faire" *Williams v. Crichton,* 84 F. 3d 581 (2d Cir 1996)

"My Mother is the Most Beautiful Woman" *Reyher v. Children's TV Workshop & Tuesday Publs.* 533 F.2d 87 (2d Cir. 1975)

Facts

Just the Facts

"Facts exist, and are not created" *Feist Publications, Inc. v. Rural Tel. Serv. Co,* 499 U.S. 340 (1991)

Rewriting History

"Copyright protection has never extended to history" *Harper & Row Publishers., v. Nation Enterprises.,* 471 U.S. 539 (1985)

The Empty Chair to the Floor of the Dinner Party

"In 1940 Marjorie Barstow Greenbie's" *Greenbie v. Hollister Noble,* 151 Fed Supp. 45 (S.D.N.Y. 1957)

"Carroll's story has since been retold" https://msa.maryland.gov/megafile/msa/specco;/sc3500/sc3520/002900/002900/html/2900bio1.html

"Anna Ella Carroll's name" https://en.wikipedia.org/wiki/List_of_women_in_the_Heritage_Floor#C

Compilations, Cookbooks, and Cowboys

"A compilation is a work" 17 U.S.C. §101

"Facts whether alone or as part" *Feist Publications, Inc. v. Rural Tel. Serv. Co,* 499 U.S. 340 (1991)

"Meredith Corporation published magazines" *Barbour v. Head,* 178 F. Supp 758 (S.D. Tex. 2002)

Useful Articles

"A "useful article" is" 17 U.S.C. §101

"Pictorial, graphic or sculptural features" Compendium of U.S. Copyright Office Practices, Third Edition, §924

"In 2016, the Supreme Court" *Star Athletica, L.L.C., v. Varsity Brands, Inc.,* 580 U.S. 1002 (2017)

Sparrows vs. Canaries

"Design Ideas, Ltd. registered a copyright" *Design Ideas, Ltd. V. Meijer, Inc.*, 2017 U.S. Dist. LEXIS 94489 (C.D. Ill. 2017)

ABC, No ©

"The ABCs are in the public domain" *Boisson v. Banian,* 273 F. 3d 262 (2d Cir. 2001)

"Typeface, typefont, lettering" 37 C.F.R. §202.1

"For example, a representation," Compendium of U.S. Copyright Office Practices, Third Edition, §906.4

"Flourishes, swirls" Compendium of U.S. Copyright Office Practices, Third Edition, §906.4

"*Star Athletica, L.L.C., v. Varsity Brands, Inc.",* 580 U.S. 1002 (2017)

"The source codes" 17 U.S.C. § 102 Compendium of U.S. Copyright Office Practices, Third Edition, §723

Graffiti, Street Art, and Copyright

"Graffiti - derived from" https:brightoneducationalfund.org/grants/springfest_art_history.htm

"Street art is often image based"   Richard September, *Graffiti v. Street Art: What is the Difference?* Graff Storm, October 2023 Available at https://graffstorm.com/graffiti-vs-street-art

"Street art is clearly copyrightable" *Castillo v. G & M Realty.,* 950 F. 3d 155 (2d Cir. 2020)

"More narrowly, graffiti" Celia Lerman *Protecting Artistic Vandalism: Graffiti and Copyright Law,* NYU Journal of Intellectual Property and Entertainment Law

"There is no definitive answer" Jamison Davies, *Art Crimes? Theoretical Perspectives on Copyright Protection for Illegally Created Graffiti Art,* 65 Maine Law Review 27 (2012) Available at https//digitalcommons.mainelawreview.edu/mlr/vol65/iss1/3

"Numerous lawsuits" Celia Lerman *Protecting Artistic Vandalism: Graffiti and Copyright Law,* NYU Journal of Intellectual Property and Entertainment Law

"Commentators often" Celia Lerman *Protecting Artistic Vandalism: Graffiti and Copyright Law,* NYU Journal of Intellectual Property and Entertainment Law

Geometric Shapes

"Common geometric shapes such as" Compendium of U.S. Copyright Office Practices, Third Edition, §906.1

"Here are some illustrations constructed" Compendium of U.S. Copyright Office Practices, Third Edition, §906.1

Colors and Coloration

"Coloration or variations in coloring alone," Compendium of U.S. Copyright Office Practices, Third Edition, §906.3

Paint it Black

"Vantablack, the blackest black" https://news.artnet.com/art-world/anish-kapoor-vantablack-2391684#:

"Vantablack, may no longer" https://news.artnet.com/art-world/stuart-semple-blackest-black-anish-kapoor-1452259

Welcome to the Public Domain

"Works that are not protected by copyright" " https://fairuse.stanford.edu/overview/public-domain/welcome/#copyright_does_not_protect_certain_works

"The public domain is the *quid pro quo*" *Sony Corp. v. Universal City Studios,* 464 U.S. 417 (1984)

"Works that are categorically ineligible" " https://fairuse.stanford.edu/overview/public-domain/welcome/#copyright_does_not_protect_certain_works

The Time Factors

"Copyright does not extend to works that were created prior to the invention of copyright" Statute of Anne, 1710, 8 Ann., c. 19 (Eng)

"Copyrights originally lasted" 57 Cong. Ch. 1-7, § 1, I Stat. 109, 110 (1790). 58 Cong. Ch. 1-15, §1, I Stat. 124 (1790)

"The unpublished and unregistered of all authors who died prior to 1933" 17 U.S.C. §300 et seq.,

"In 1998, the Sonny Bono Copyright Term Extension Act" https://www.copyright.gov/pr/pdomain.html" 17 U.S.C. §§ 302, 304 *Eldred v. Ashcroft,* 587 U.S. 186 (2003)

"As a result, Steamboat Willie" https://www.authorsalliance.org/2022/05/25/copyright-term-disney-and-steamboat-willie/

"Caution: The Mickeys" See Trademarks: Slogan Mottos, etc., supra.

"Copyright scholars" See, for example, Jessica Jenkins, *In Ambiguous Battle , The Promise and Pathos pf Public Domain Day , 2014* https://scholarship.law.duke.edu/cgi/viewcontent.cgi?referer=&httpsredir=1&article=1244&context=dlt

In or Out of the Pool

"Figuring out what is or is not" https://guides.library.cornell.edu/copyright/publicdomain

The EXCLUSIVE RIGHTS of Copyright

Introducing the Bundle of Rights

"The invention of the printing press" https://www.loc.gov/item/myloc8/

The first copyright law, the Statute of Anne" Statute of Anne, 1710, 8 Ann., c. 19 (Eng)

"Over the years, additional rights have been formulated" *Mazer v. Stein,* 347 U.S. 201 (1954)

"The Copyright Act of 1976" 17 U.S.C. §101 et seq.

This Act was motivated in part" *ABC, Inc. v. Aereo, Inc.,* 573 U.S. 431 (2014)

The Current Bundle of Rights

"The Copyright Act of 1976" 17 U.S.C. § 100, et seq.

Renegotiation of the Social Bargain and the Internet Treaties

"This foundational shift" 1 WIPO Copyright Treaty art. 8, Dec. 20, 1996, 36 I.L.M. 65 (1997) ("WCT"); *see also* WIPO Performances and Phonograms Treaty arts. 10, 14, Dec. 20, 1996, 36 I.L.M. 76 (1997) ("WPPT").

"The information age raises issues at the heart of copyright's social bargain" http//www.wipo.int/about-wipo/en/dgo/speeches/dg-blueskyconf_1

"Under the umbrella solution" Mihály Ficsor, *International Harmonization of Copyright and Neighboring Rights, in* WIPO Worldwide Symposium on Copyright in the Global Information Infrastructure, 374 (WIPO Pub. No. 746 (E/S), 1995).U.S.© 45 U.S. © 43.

"The making available right is technology neutral" *The Making Available Right in the United States,* A Report of the Register of Copyrights, 2016, p.1

"The United States has consistently maintained" *The Making Available Right in the United States,* A Report of the Register of Copyrights, 2016, p.1

"Some judges and scholars disagree" Ken Nicholds, *The Free Jammie Movement: Is Making a File Available to Other users Over a Peer-to-Peer Computer Network Sufficient to Infringe the Copyright Owner's 17 U.S.C. § 106(3) Distribution Right?,* 78 Fordham L. Rev. 983 (2009). (Available at: https://ir.lawnet.fordham.edu/flr/vol78/iss2/14)

Moving forward

"The exclusive rights are cumulative" 17 U.S.C. §106

Divide and Conquer

"The exclusive rights can be subdivided" 17 U.S.C. §201 (d) (1)

Go Forth and Multiply: Reproduction Rights and Copyright

"The first right" 17.U.S.C. §106(1)

Defining Copy

"In everyday usage" www.oxfordlearnersdictionaries.com/U.S./definition/english/copy

A "copy" is defined" 17 U.S.C. §101

Some Copies in the Copyright Sense

"The seminal example" Melville Nimmer & David Nimmer, *Nimmer of Copyright: A Treatise on the Law of Literary, Musical and Artistic Property,* §8.02, The Reproduction Right

"Artist Lee Teter" *Teter v. Glass Onion, Inc.,* 723 F. Supp. 2d 1138 (W.D. Missouri 2010)

Phonorecords in the Copyright Sense

"Like copy, phonorecord" 17 U.S.C. §101, See, *London Sire Records v. Doe,* 542 F. Supp. 153,171 (D.Mass. 2008)

"Although visual art is not reproduced" *Capitol Records v. ReDigi* 910 F.3d 649 (2d Cir. 2018)

Caution: Private Copies are Copies

"Copies of webpages stored" *Ticketmaster LLC v. RMG Technologies, Inc.,* 507 F. Supp. 2d 1096 (C.D. Cal. 2007) *Cartoon Network LP, LLP v. CSC Holdings, Inc.,* 536 F.3d 121 (2d Cir. 2008)

There are Limits

"There are also numerous, narrow" 17 U.S.C. §§108,112,113,114,115,117,121, 121A

The Right to Make Derivative Works

On the Meta Level

"In the grand scheme of things" *Emerson v. Davies,* 8 F.Case 615, 3 Story, 768, 4 West Law J. 261, 8 Law Rep. 27- (D)

In Copyright Law

"The right to make derivative works" 17 U.S.C. §106 (2)

"A change in the medium" Pierre N. Leval, *Campbell as Fair Use Blueprint?,* 90 Wash. L. Rev. 597 (2015). Available at: https://digitalcommons.law.uw.edu/wlr/vol90/iss2/3

A Sticky Situation

"Antioch Company was the copyright owner" *Antioch Co., v. Scrapbook Borders, Inc.,* 291 F.Supp 2d 980 (D. Minn. 2003)

Guitars + Symbols

"The artist formerly known as Prince" *Pickett v. Prince,* 207 F. 3d 402 (7th Cir. 2000)

Derivative Work v. Fair Use

'Fair use is the right" Pierre N. Leval, *Campbell as Fair Use Blueprint?,* 90 Wash. L. Rev. 597 (2015). Available at: https://digitalcommons.law.uw.edu/wlr/vol90/iss2/3

"Defendants in infringement lawsuits" *Rogers v. Koons,* 960 F. 2d 301 (2d Cir. 1992) *Harpers & Row Publishers. v Nation Enters.* 471 U.S. 539 (1985)

Derivative Works: The Sequel

"Sequels are derivative works" Nimmer on Copyright 2.12

"FormGen, Inc. owned the right" *Microstar v. FormGen, Inc.,* 154 F.3d 1107 (9th Cir. 1998)

Characters Are Copyrightable

"*Cartoons and comic strips*" U.S. Copyright Office Circular 44, *Cartoons and Comic Strips*

A Few Words about Fan Art + Fan Fiction

"Fan art is a drawing" https://en.wikipedia.org/wiki/Fan_art

"Fan fiction uses established characters" https://en.wikipedia.org/wiki/Fan_fiction

"The copyright owners of popular and profitable" Madhavi Sunder, *When Fandom Clashes with IP Law,* Harvard Business Review, July 23, 2019 (Available at: https://hbr.org/2019/07/when-fandom-clashes-with-ip-law)

"For example, when Axanar Productions" *Paramount Pictures Corp. v. Axanar Prods., Inc.* Case No. 2:2015cv09938

"In very few instances, See Section V, Fair Use, infra.

"As part of the settlement" https://www.theverge.com/2017/1/20/14340666/axanar-productions-settled-lawsuit-paramount-star-trek-fanfilm.

A Short History

"The display right is the most recent" *Burwood Prods. Co. v. Marsel Mirror & Glass Prods.,* 468 F. Supp. 1215 (N.D. Ill. 1979)

Initially, the expansive scope of the copy" R. Anthony Reese, *The Public Display Right: The Copyright Act's Neglected Solution to the Controversy Over RAM "Copies"* 2001 University of Illinois Law Review 83 (2001)

Defining Display

"The exclusive right" 17 U.S.C. §106(5)

"The definition of display" 17 U.S.C. §101

Some parameters

"The display right applies to the visual arts" 17 U.S.C. §106(5)

"Only unauthorized displays made publicly" 17 U.S C. §101

The Server Test

"The online unauthorized showing of nude photographs" *Perfect 10 v. Amazon.com, Inc.,* 508 F. 3d 1146 (9th Cir. 2007)

Other Views on Display

"Not all courts who have looked" *The Leader's Inst., LLC v. Jackson 2017 U.S. DIst LEXIS 193555 (N.D. Tex. 2017)*

"Justin Goldman's copyrighted photo of football legend Tom Brady" *Goldman v. Breitbart News,* 302 F. Supp. 3d 585 (S.D.N.Y. 2018)

A Cautionary Tale

"When Stephanie Sinclair, another professional photographer" *Sinclair v. Ziff Davis, LLC,* 454 F. Supp. 3d 342 (S.D.N.Y. 2020)

"Instagram revised its terms" https://help.instagram.com/581066165581870

On Display in the Material World

"Most common place real world displays" 17 U.S C. §109(c)

"Oddly, this exception also extends to the projection of an image" 17 U.S C. §101

"A case that has been described as "the ultimate how-not-to guide" *Mass. Museum of Contemporary Art Found., Inc. v. Buchel,* 593 F.3d 38 (1st Cir. 2010)

The Performance Right

"The performance right applies" 17 U.S C. §106(4)

"The interplay between judicial interpretation" *ABC, Inc. v. Aereo, Inc.,* 573 U.S. 431 (2014)

The Transmit Clause

"The Transmit Clause in the Copyright Act of 1976 was added" *ABC, Inc. v. Aereo, Inc.,* 573 U.S. 431 (2014)

"The Transmit Clause provides" 17 U.S C. §101

Private Antennae, Public Performances

"Aereo, Inc. used a system" *ABC, Inc. v. Aereo, Inc.,* 573 U.S. 431 (2014)

One at a Time

"Aereo's argument that because personal antennas" *ABC, Inc. v. Aereo, Inc.,* 573 U.S. 431 (2014)

If it Quacks Like a Duck

"Aereo maintained that it was different" *ABC, Inc. v. Aereo, Inc.,* 573 U.S. 431 (2014)

Performance Rights Organizations

"A complex statutory framework" 17 U.S.C. §115

"This area is beyond the scope" https://www.rocknrolllaw.com/product/the-musicians-guide-to-music-copyright-law

Not for Profit, Not a Defense

"But it's for charity" 17 U.S.C. §110

The Distribution Right

A Long History

"Historically, the dissemination of" Jane C Ginsburg, '*From Having Copies to Experiencing Works: The Development of an Access Right in U.S. Copyright Law*' 50 J Copyright Soc 113 (2003)

"Previously, U.S. copyright law provided copyright owners" Copyright Act of 1909, §106

"Since 1976 copyright owners" 17 U.S.C. §106(3)

"There are some holes in its coverage. "Ken Nicholds, *The Free Jammie Movement: Is Making a File Available to Other Users Over a Peer-to-Peer Computer Network Sufficient to Infringe the Copyright Owner's 17 U.S.C. § 106(3) Distribution Right?,* 78 Fordham L. Rev. 983 (2009). (Available at: https://ir.lawnet.fordham.edu/flr/vol78/iss2/14)

Defining the Distribution Right

"A copyright owner has the exclusive right" 17 U.S.C. §106(3)

It's (im)Material

"How phonorecords play out" *London-Sire Records Inc., v Doe,* 542 F. Supp. 2d 153 (D Mass 2008).

Public Distribution

"Only distribution to the public" 17 U.S.C. §106(3)

Right of First Publication

"In addition to giving the copyright owner" *Harper & Row, Publishers, Inc. v. Nation Enters.,* 471 U.S. 539 (1985)

Transfers of Ownership

"The exclusive right applies only" 17 U.S.C. §106(3)

"Typically, when a digital file" *London-Sire Records Inc v Doe,* 542 F. Supp. 2d 153 (D Mass 2008).

Actually, or Not

"The courts and commentators consistently agree that when a public library" *Hotaling v. Church of Jesus Christ of Latter Day Saints,* 118 F. 3d 199 (4th Cir. 1997)

"This consistency deteriorates in the digital domain" "Ken Nicholds, *The Free Jammie Movement: Is Making a File Available to Other Users Over a Peer-to-Peer Computer Network Sufficient to Infringe the Copyright Owner's 17 U.S.C. § 106(3) Distribution Right?,* 78 Fordham L. Rev. 983 (2009). (Available at: https://ir.lawnet.fordham.edu/flr/vol78/iss2/14)

"Napster started providing" *A&M Records v. Napster, Inc.,* 239 F. 3d 1004 (9th Cir. 2001)

"Some courts have held that an online offer" See, e.g., *Malibu Media, LLC v. Dhandapani,* 2020 U.S. Dist. LEXIS 194794, (N.D. Tex. Feb. 12, 2020) ; *Universal City Studios Prods. LLP v. Bigwood*, 441 F. Supp. 2d 185 (D. Me. 2006); *Arista Records LLC v. Greubel*, 453 F. Supp. 2d 961 (N.D. Tex. 2006); *Motown Record Co. v. DePietro,* 2007 U.S. Dist. LEXIS 11626 (E.D. Pa. Feb. 20, 2007).

"Other courts have held evidence of an actual download" See, e.g., At*lantic Recording Corp. v. Howell,* 554 F. Supp. 2d 976, 981 (D. Ariz. 2008); *Capitol Records, Inc. v. Thomas*, 579 F. Supp. 2d 1210, 1225 (D. Minn. 2008); *BMG Rights Mgmt. (U.S.) LLC v. Cox Commc'ns, Inc.*, 149 F. Supp. 3d 634 (E.D. Va. 2015), aff'd in part, rev'd in part, 881 F.3d 293 (4th Cir. 2018)

"This inconsistency" Gaetano Dimitra *The WIPO Right of Making Available* Research Handbook on Copyright Law, Chapter 6, 2017 (Available at: https://qmro.qmul.ac.uk/xmlui/handle/123456789/54834)

In or Out

"Importation into the United States" 17 U.S.C. §602

The First Sale Doctrine

One and Done

"The first sale doctrine provides a defense" 17 U.S.C. §109(a)

"After the title of a work is transferred by" *Kirtsaeng v. John Wiley & Sons, Inc.* 568 U.S. 519 (2013)

"Libraries, used book" *Kirtsaeng v. John Wiley & Sons, Inc.* 568 U.S. 519 (2013)

Narrow Application

"It applies only to the actual physical work" 17 U.S.C. §202

"For example, in ReDigi" *Capital Records. LLC v. ReDigi Inc.,* 910 F 3d 649 (2d Cir. 2018)

"The first sale doctrine does, however, extend" *Kirtsaeng v. John Wiley & Sons, Inc.* 568 U.S. 519 (2013)

Resale Royalties, Not Yet

"An artist royalty, or *droit de suite*" See generally U.S. Copyright Office, Droit de Suite: *The Artist's Resale Royalty* (Dec. 1992) ("1992 Copyright Report"); U.S. Copyright Office, *Resale Royalties: An Updated Analysis* (Dec. 2013) ("2013 Copyright Report")

"Resale royalties are not currently included" 17 U.S.C. §106

California Dreaming

"In 1977, California enacted" *Close v. Sotheby's, Inc.,* 894 F. 3d 1061 (9th Cir. 2018)

NFTs

"NFTs typically provide" James Howell, *NFT Royalties Explained* available at https://101blockchains.com/nft-royalties-explained/#

"The tokens are blockchained based"   Rakesh Sharma, *Non-Fungible Token (NFT): What It Means And How It Works,* https://www.investopedia.com/non-fungible-tokens-nft-5115211

"Fungible" https://www.law.cornell.edu/wex/fungible_things

"Blockchain is" Emily Rutland, *Blockchain Byte,* available at https://www.finra.org/sites/default/files/2017_BC_Byte.pdfBlockchain Byte

Licenses

"Licenses, like provisions for resale royalties" *NFT Standards Wiki* https://www.nftstandards.wtf/NFT/NFT+License#:~:text

"For example, cryptokitties" https://medium.com/dapperlabs/nft-license-2-0-why-a-nft-can-do-what-mickey-mouse-never-could-27673d5f29aa

"An NFT with a digital image of Basquiat's" https://www.artforum.com/news/basquiat-nft-pulled-from-auction-after-sparking-controversy-249825/

VARA

Droit Moral

"Droit moral" is a French term" https://cyber.harvard.edu/property/library/moralprimer.

VARA Overview

"Droit moral has limited application" 17 U.S.C. §106A

5 Pointz

5 Pointz in Long Island City" *Castillo v. G & M Realty.,* 950 F. 3d 155 (2d Cir. 2020)

The OWNERSHIP of Copyright

The Ownership of Copyright

"As a general rule, copyright ownership belongs" 17 U.S.C. §201

An Overview of Ownership

Authors or Proprietors

"The very first copyright statute" Statute of Anne, 1710, 8 Ann., c. 19 (Eng)

"The U.S. Constitution gives Congress" U.S. Constitution, 1789 Art. I, Sect. 8, Cl. 8)

"This use continues" 17 U.S.C. §201

Learned Men and Pseudonymous Women

"Copyright itself was created" Statute of Anne, 1710, 8 Ann., c. 19 (Eng)

"Although there has never been a requirement" https://artuk.org/discover/stories/ten-women-who-U.S.ed-pseudonyms-and-one-man

"June Tarpe Mills" https://en.wikipedia.org/wiki/June_Tarp%C3%A9_Mills"

" Elaine de Koonig" https://en.wikipedia.org/wiki/Elaine_de_Kooning

"A work registered under a pseudonym" 17 U.S.C. §302 (c)

"Other copyrights span" 17 U.S.C. §302 (a)

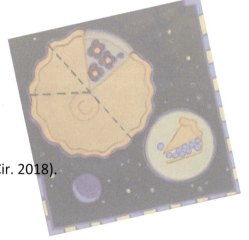

Citizenship

"You do not need to be a U.S. citizen" U.S. Copyright Circular 38A

"All UNpubished copyrightable works" 17 U.S.C. §104(a)

"Some examples of points of attachment" 17 U.S.C. §104(b) (1), (2)

Animals Need Not Apply

"In 2011, nature photographer" *Naruto v. Slater,* 888 F.3d 418 (9th Cir. 2018).

"In 1879" *The Trademark Cases,* 100 U.S. 82 (1879)

Deus ex Machina

"The U.S. Copyright Office will not" Compendium of U.S. Copyright Office Practices, Third Edition, §312

People not Machines

" "Writings" must be" *The Trademark Cases,* 100 U.S. 82 (1879)

"Machines cannot be authors" Compendium of U.S. Copyright Office Practices, Third Edition, §313

Artificial Intelligence Is (Not)

"AI is defined" https://csrc.nist.gov/Topics/technologies/artificial-intelligence#:

"Margaret Boden," Boden, Margaret A. , *Artificial Intelligence: A Very Short Introduction,* Oxford University Press (2018)

BIG Questions and Copyright Issues

The Output

"AI generated visual art" copyright.gov/zarya-of-the-dawn

"Authorship has traditionally" See Who Can be an Author, supra.

Zarya of the Dawn + The U.S. Copyright Office Answer

"After Kristina Kashtanova, obtained a copyright registration" copyright.gov/zarya-of-the-dawn

"The Copyright Office's denial" *Thaler v. Perlmutter*, _ F. Supp. 3d _, 2023 WL 5333236, at *10 (D.D.C. Aug. 18, 2023).

"The Copyright Office now requires" Copyright Registration Guidance: Works Containing Material Generated by Artificial Intelligence March 16, 2023, 16190 Federal Register, Vol. 88, No. 51 Rules and Regulations, 37 CFR Part 202.

How Much is Enough?

"Jason Allen's input" Copyright Office Review Board decision 9/6/2023

Some OBVIOUSly Different Answers

"Obvious, a French collective" https://obvious-art.com/page-about-obvious/#:~:text

"The UK takes a similar approach" https://www.privacyworld.blog/2023/07/copyright-protection-for-ai-works-uk-vs-us

"Karla Saldana Ochoa " C:\Users\User\Dropbox\My PC (DESKTOP- 90GVU3)\Documents\Webinars\AI\Can AI mark the next Architectural Revolution_ _ by Urban AI _ Urban AI _ Medium.mhtml

Input: What feeds AI? Does it Infringe Copyrights?

"Scraping" https://www.dazeddigital.com/art-photography/article/57996/1/what-ai-image-scraping-how-can-artists-fight-back-meta-getty-stable-diffusion

License to Train

"Consent, Credit, Compensation" https://www.washingtonpost.com/technology/2023/07/16/ai-programs-training-lawsuits-fair-use/

"Copyright owners have begun to" https://copyrightalliance.org/copyrighted-works-training-ai-fair-use/

Q: Fair Use?

A: It Depends

"Fair use is the right" Cala Coffman, *Does the Use of Copyrighted Work Qualify as a Fair Use?*, https://copyrightalliance.org/copyrighted-works-training-ai-fair-use/

Moving Forward

Collaborations, Co-Authors, Commissions, and Compilations

"Collaborations have also led to a lot of lawsuits" See e.g. *Aalmuhammed v. Lee*, 202 F.3d 1227 (9th Cir. 2000); *Greene v. Ablon*, 794 F. 3d 133 (1st Cir. 2015); *Brownstein v. Lindsay*, 742 F. 3d 55 (1st Cir. 2014) and other cases cited herein.

"Co-authors are co-owners" 17 U.S.C. §201

The Statutory Framework

"Copyright ownership vests" 17 U.S.C. §201

Defining Lines

"A joint work is defined as" 17 U.S.C. §101

"Generally, technical roles like editors" *Gaylord v. United States,* 595 F.3d 1364 (Fed. Cir. 2010); *Erickson v. Trinity Theatre, Inc.*, 13 F.3d 1061 (7th Cir. 1994); *S.O.S., Inc. v. Payday, Inc.,* 886 F.2d 1081 (9th Cir. 1989)

Intent: To be, or Not to be, a Co-Author

"The intent of collaborators to be co-authors" *Childress v. Taylor,* 945 F.2d 500 (2d Cir. 1991),

"If there is no agreement, " *Thomson v. Larson,* 147 F.3d 195 (2d Cir. 1998).

Nature of the Contribution: Copyrightable or Not

'First, the minority rule" *Greene v. Ablon,* 794 F.3d 133 (1st Cir. 2015) *Brownstein v. Lindsay*, 742 F.3d 55, 64 (3d Cir. 2014)

"Next, the majority rule" *Janky v. Lake County Convention & Visitors Bureau*, 576 F.3d 356, (7th Cir. 2009), *Thomson v. Larson* 147 F 3d 195 (2d Cir. 1998), *Ashton-Tate v. Ross,* 916 F.2d 516, (9th Cir. 1990) *M.G.B. Homes v. Ameron Homes, Inc.* 903 F. 2d 1496 (11th Cir. 1990).

'Now, the exception to the majority rule" *Gaiman v. McFarlane*, 360 F. 3d 644 (7th Cir. 2004)

A Comic Book Case Study

"Todd McFarlane, a writer" *Gaiman v. McFarlane,* 360 F. 3d 644 (7th Cir. 2004)

Co-Ownership of the Count

"McFarlane asked Gaiman" *Gaiman v. McFarlane,* 360 F. 3d 644 7th Cir. 2004)

Medieval Spawn

"Medieval Spawn was a closer case" *Gaiman v. McFarlane,* 360 F. 3d 644 (7th Cir. 2004)

The Consequences of Co-Authorship

"Co-authors are co-owners of the copyright in a joint work." 17 U.S.C. §201, *Childress v. Taylor,* 945 F.2d 500 (2d Cir. 1991),

"Each co-author may distribute" *Weinstein v. University of Illinois,* 811 F.2d 1091 (7th Cir. 1987).

Royalties are Different

"Royalties are compensation" https://www.law.cornell.edu/wex/royalty#:~:text=

Works Made for Hire

What are Works Made for Hire?

" 'Works made for hire' is a term" 17 U.S.C. §101

Works Created by Employees in the Scope of Employment

"Here are some examples" *Committee for Creative Non-Violence v. Reid,* 490 US 730 (1989)

The Second Situation

"For copyright ownership to vest" 17 U.S.C. §101

"Here is the list of types of works with a bit of amplification" U.S. Copyright Office, *Circular 30, Works Made For Hire* Available at https://www.copyright.gov/circs/circ30.pdf

There Are Consequences

" The author of a work made for hire is the employer" 17 U.S.C. §201(b)

" A party that special commissions a work" *Committee for Creative Non-Violence v. Reid,* 490 US 730 2166 (1989)

"The life span and availability of termination rights" 17 U.S.C. §§203, 304

"To sort out whether" U.S. Copyright Office, *Circular 30, Works Made For Hire* Available at https://www.copyright.gov/circs/circ30.pdf

7 Questions

Assignments/Transfers

Introduction

"The copyright is retained" 17 U.S.C. §202

"Copyrights can be bought, sold" 17 U.S.C. §201(d)

What is an Assignment?

"Assignments are a way to transfer" ttps://www.law.cornell.edu/wex/assignment#:

"Assignments must be in writing" 17 U.S.C. §204 (a)

Licenses

Why Use a License?

"Licenses do not transfer ownership" *Gardner v. Nike,* 279 F.3d 774 (9th Cir. 2002)

License This, License That

"The right to use copyrighted material" 17 U.S.C. §201(d)

How to Create a License

"There are three ways to create a license" *Jarrod Maxwell, Inc. v. Veeck,* 110 F.3d 749 (11th Cir. 1997)

By Implication

"Implied licenses are created" *Latimer v. Roaring Toyz*, 601 F. 3d 1224 (11th Cir. 2010)

"The 11th Circuit found" *Latimer v. Roaring Toyz*, 601 F. 3d 1224 (11th Cir. 2010)

"Another court, found that a photographer" *McElroy v. Ajinca Events, LLC* 512 F. Supp 3d 1328 (N.D. Ga 2021)

CopyLEFT

"The copyleft movement is on a mission to provide alternatives to copyright" https://pitt.libguides.com/copyright/licenses

"In 1989, GNU created" www.gnu.org/copyleft

Creative Commons

"In 2002, Creative Commons developed" www.creativecommons.org

"CC licenses are used" https://en.wikipedia.org/wiki/Creative_Commons

3 Things, 4 Components, and 6+ Licenses

"Three important things to know" https://creativecommons.org

The Creative Commons (CC) Licenses are" www.creativecommons.org

It is Forever, for Some

"CC licenses are irrevocable" " https://creativecommons.org/licenses/by/4.0/legalcode

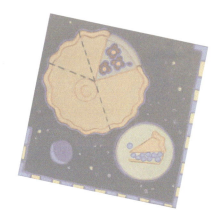

The FAIR USE Doctrine

The Fair Use Doctrine

A Fair Use Tale

"In 1440, the world changed" https://www.loc.gov/item/myloc8/

"In 1710, the Statute of Anne" Statute of Anne, 1710, 8 Ann., c. 19 (Eng)

1741: The Origin Story

"In 1741, the doctrine of fair use" *Gyles v. Wilcox,* (1741) 26 Eng. Rep. 489 (Ch.)

"Abridgement, the process of making" Deazley, R. (2008) '*Commentary on Gyles v. Wilcox (1741)*', in *Primary Sources on Copyright (1450-1900),* eds L. Bently & M. Kretschmer, www.copyrighthistory.org; Available at: https://pure.qub.ac.uk/en/publications/commentary-on-gyles-v-wilcox-1741; C.L. Carlson, *The First Magazine: A History of the Gentlemen's Magazine* (Providence, Brown University, 1938

1841: Fair Abridgement Comes to the U.S.

"Copyright law in the United States" Art I, Sec. 8, U.S. Constitution

"Folsom published *The Writings of George Washington,*" *Folsom v. Marsh,* 9 F. Cas. 342 (C.C.D. Mass. 1841)

1976: Fair Use Codified

"In 1976, the fair use doctrine became a statute" 17 U.S.C. §107

1990: Toward a Standard Standard

"Important publishers" role. Kenneth A. Plevan, *The Second Circuit + the Development of Intellectual Property*

Law: The First 125 Years, 85 Fordham L. Rev. 143 (2016) William K. Ford, *Judging Experience in Copyright Law,* 14, J. Intell. Prop. L., 1,41 (2006).

"Some of his decisions" *New Era Publications v. Henry Holt & Co.,* 695 F. Supp. 1493 (S.D.N.Y. 1988) *aff'd* 873 F.2d 576 (2d Cir. 1989): *Salinger v. Random House,* 650 F. Supp. 413 (S.D.N.Y. 1986) *rev'd* 811 F. 2d 90 (2d Circ. 1987) *cert. denied,* 484 U.S. 890 (1987);

"This spurred Judge Leval" Pierre N. Leval, *Toward A Fair Use Standard,* 103 Harvard Law Review 1105 (1993)

"Judge Leval's commentary" *Campbell v. Acuff Rose Music, Inc.,* 510 U.S. 569 (1994)

1994: Pretty/Nasty Transformation

"The U.S. Supreme Court disagreed" *Campbell v. Acuff Rose Music, Inc.,* 510 U.S. 569 (1994)

2021: Round Peg, Square Hole. No Locks.

"Some judges have complained" *Lotus Development Corp. v. Borland Int'l, Inc.,* 49 F. 3d 807 (CA1 1995) (Boudin, J., concurring).

"In Google v. Oracle the Supreme Court" 593 U.S. (2021); 141 S.Ct 1183, (2021)

Fair Use, The Statute

"The factors developed by the courts" 17 U.S.C. §107

"Fair use is an affirmative defense" https://www.law.cornell.edu/wex/affirmative_defense#:~

The Four Statutory Factors

"To determine whether a use" 17 U.S.C. §107 (1) –(4)

"The fasctors are not exclusive" https://www.copyright.gov/fair-U.S.e/

"The factors are to be weighed together" *Video Pipeline, Inc. v. Buena Vista Home Entm't, Inc.,* 342 F.3d 19 (3d Cir. 2003)

"Historically, but not always" Barton Beebe, *An Empirical Study of U.S. Copyright Fair U.S.e Opinions Updated, 1978-2019,* 10 NYU Journal of Intellectual Property & Entertainment Law 1

"There are no bright line rules" *Blanch v. Koons,* 467 F. 3d 244 (2d Cir. 2006)

"The ultimate question" *Castle Rock Entm't, Inc. v. Carol Publ'g,* 150 F.2d 132 (2d Cir.1998)

The First Factor

"The first factor is" 17 U.S.C. §107 (1)

"Original copyrightable expressions" *Castle Rock Entm't, Inc. v. Carol Publ'g,* 150 F.2d 132 (2d Cir.1998)

Making Fun

"A parody is" *Campbell v. Acuff Rose Music, Inc.,* 510 U.S. 569 (1994)

Money Isn't Everything

"Use for non-profit educational purposes" Pierre N. Leval, *Toward A Fair Use Standard,* 103 Harvard Law Review 1105 (1993)

"Commercial uses can be fair uses." *Campbell v. Acuff Rose Music, Inc.,* 510 U.S. 569 (1994)

"Criticism, commentary, research" 17 U.S.C. §107

"Bad faith, like commerciality" Eva Subotnik. *Intent in Fair Use,* 18 Lewis & Clark Law Review 935 (2014) Available at: https://law.lclark.edu/law_reviews/lewis_and_clark_law_review/past_issues/volume_18/volume-18-number-4-2014/

Warhol v. Goldsmith

"In *Andy Warhol Foundation v. Goldsmith*" 598 U.S.__(2023)

In their opinion(s)

Dissenting opinions, like concurring opinions" "https://www.law.cornell.edu/wex/dissenting_opinion#:

"Dissents appeal" Charles Hughes, The Supreme Court of the United States 68 (1936)

"Dissents contribute " Hon. Ruth Bader Ginsburg, *The Role of Dissenting Opinions,* Minnesota Law Review 95:1 2020

Take away

"An increase in licensing" Peter J. Karol, *The Transformative Impact of Warhol v. Goldsmith,* Art Guide, June 2023, Available at https://www.artforum.com/columns/the-transformative-impact-of-_warhol-v-goldsmith_-252757/

Transformative, For Example

"Andrea Blanch, an accomplished photographer" *Blanch v. Koons,* 467 F. 3d 244 (2d Cir. 2006)

"Jeff Koons, is one of the most prominent" https://www.artnews.com/feature/jeff-koons-career-milestones-1202683827/; www.jeffkoons.com

The Second Factor

"The second factor is" 17 U.S.C. §107 (2)

"Facts, ideas, methods fall outside" See Subject Matter at pages

"Information about current events" *International News Services v. Associated Press.* 248 U.S. 215 (1918), *Harper & Row Publrs., v. Nation Enters.,* 471 U.S. 539 (1991)

"Computer programs almost always" *Google v. Oracle,* 593 U.S. (2021), 141 S.Ct. 1183 (2021)

"Roy Orbison's Pretty Woman lyrics" *Campbell v. Acuff Rose Music, Inc.,* 510 U.S. 569 (1994)

"Andrea Blanch's glamorous photograph" *Blanch v. Koons,* 467 F. 3d 244 (2d Cir. 2006)

"Many of the works copied by Google in its Library Project were fiction" *Author's Guild v. Google,* 804 F 3d 202 (2d Cir. 2014)

"This is an infringement of the author's exclusive right" *Harper & Row Publrs., v. Nation Enters.,* 471 U.S. 539 (1991) *Zacchini v. Scripps-Howard Broadcasting Co..* 433 U.S. 562 (1977)

The Third Factor

"The third fact to be considered is" 17 U.S.C. §107 (3)

"The clear implication" *Author's Guild v. Google,* 804 F.3d 202 (2d Cir 2015)

No Formula – Really

"Despite a persistent urban myth" https://copyright.gov/fair-use/

The Heart of the Matter

"President Gerald Ford granted former President Nixon" https://www.archivesfoundation.org/documents/Richard-nixon-resignation-letter-gerald-ford-pardon/

"Even though The Nation" *Harper & Row Publrs., v. Nation Enters.,* 471 U.S. 539 1991)

"The Supreme Court has consistently held" *Golan v. Holder,* 565 U.S. 302(2011)

The Whole Thing

"Dorling Kindersley ("DK Publishing") published" *Bill Graham Archives v Doring Kindersley Ltd.,* 448 F. 3d 605 (2d Cir. 2006)

The Fourth Factor

"The fourth factor is" 17 U.S.C. §107(4)

"This factor is undoubtedly the single most important element" *Capitol Records, LLC v. ReDigi Inc.,* 910 F. 3d 649 (2d Cir. 2018)

Pictures, Purpose and Profit

"Lawrence Schwartzwald photographed" *Schwartzwald v. Oath, Inc.,* 2020 LEXIS 165641 (S.D.N.Y. 2020)

Go-to-Market

"The right to make derivative works" 17 U.S.C. §106(2)

Do Not Pass Go!

"Dr. Seuss's last book" *Dr. Seuss Entrs., L.P. v ComicMix LLC*, 983 F.3d 443 (9th Cir. 2020)

"A mash-up is" https://www.merriam-webster.com/dictionary/mash-up

Criticism is Encouraged

"Although biting criticism" *Campbell v. Acuff Rose Music, Inc.,* 510 U.S. 569 (1994)

All Together Now

"Fair Use is a holistic, context sensitive inquiry" *Campbell v. Acuff Rose Music, Inc.,* 510 U.S. 569 (1994)

"The four statutory fair use factors are weighed" Pierre N. Leval, *Campbell as a Fair Use Blueprint?,* 90 Wash. L. Rev. 597 (2015); Available at: https://digitalcommons.law.uw.edu/wlr/vol90/iss2/3

Four More (Stories NOT Factors)

Brammer v. Violent Hues Productions LLV 922 F. 3d 255 (4th Cir. 2019)

Blanche v. Koons, 467 F. 3d 244 (2d Cir. 2006)

Noland v. Janssen, 2020 U.S. Dist LEXIS 95454 (S.D.N.Y. 2020)

Konangataa v. Am. Broadcasting Companies, 2017 U.S. Dist. LEXIS (S.D.N.Y. 2017)

The LEGAL CARE AND PROTECTION of Copyright

Giving Your Notice

"You are automatically the owner" 17 U.S.C. §201

"Although copyright notices have not been required" U.S. Copyright Notice, Circular 3, *Copyright Notice* Available at: https://www.copyright.gov/circs/circ03.pdf

The Elements of Notice

"A copyright notice has three elements" 17 U.S.C. §401(b)

Where to Put It

"For paintings, prints, photographs" 17 U.S.C. §401(c)

Starting with Why

"Federal copyright protection starts" 17 U.S.C. §201

"A work must be registered" *Fourth Estate Public Benefit Corp., v. Wall-street.com LLC,* 138 S.Ct. 881 (2019)

"A small claims proceeding" 17 U.S.C. §1505

Registration DIY

"The U.S. Copyright Office strongly encourages" U.S. Copyright Office, Circular 2, *Copyright Registration* Available at: https://www.copyright.gov/circs/circ02.pdf

The Application

"The basic registration forms include:" https://www.copyright.gov/forms/

"Form VA contains the basic information" https://www.copyright.gov/forms/formva.pdf

Author(s)

Creation and Publication

"Basically, publication means" 17 U.S.C. §101

"Prior to 1989" *Letter Edged in Black Press, Inc. v. Public Bldg. Com.,* 320 F. Supp. 1303 (N.D. Ill 1970)

Safe Harbors and Help

"Making an inadvertent mistake" *Unicolors, Inc. v. H & M Hennes & Mauritz, LLP,* 142 S. Ct. 941 (2022)f

$ x $ x $ = Money and Multiples

"Single author, same claimant" U.S. Copyright Office, Circular 4 , *Copyright Office Fees* Available at:

"One option to cut" U.S. Copyright Office, Circular 34, *Multiple Works* Available at: https://www.copyright.gov/circs/circ34.pdf

"Photographers can" U.S. Copyright Office, Circular 42 , *Copyright Registration of Photographs;* Available at https://www.copyright.gov/circs/circ42.pdf

Deposit Copies Are Not Mandatory Deposits

"For visual arts or three-dimensional works" U.S. Copyright Office, Circular 40A, *Deposit Requirements of*

Claims to Copyright in Visual Arts Material, Available at: https://www.copyright.gov/circs/circ40a.pdf

"Copyright owners have been required to submit" Steven Gillen, *What You Need To Know About Copyright Mandatory Deposit, IPBA Independent* Magazine, October 2016; Available at: https://articles.ibpa-online.org/article/need-know-copyright-mandatory-deposit/

"For works published in the United States" 17 U.S. §408(b)

Infringement

What is Copyright Infringement?

What Do You Have to Prove?

"There are two core elements" *Feist Publ'ns v. Rural Tel. Serv. Co.,* 490 9 U.S. 340 (1991)

You Have to Own It

"You must first prove you own the copyright" 17 U.S. §501(b)

"Registration is also required before an infringement lawsuit" *Fourth Estate Public Benefit Corp., v. Wall-street.com LLC,* 138 S.Ct. 881 (2019)

Pink Coats, Piggy Backs

"Donald A. Harney, a freelance photographer," *Harney v. Sony Pictures TV, Inc.,* 704 F. 3d 173 (1st Cir. 2013) 17 U.S. §501(b)

Cease and Desist!

"Cease and desist letters should include" *Copyright Cease and Desist Letters,* LEXIS Practical Guidance, maintained by Laura M. King, Matrix Law Group LLP

"Cease and desist letters have pros and cons" *Presuit Considerations in Copyright Litigation,* LEXIS Practical Guidance, maintained by Scott J. Sholder and Elizabeth Altman, Cowan, DeBaets, Abrahams & Sheppard LLP

Lawsuits

"If you are able to prove that your copyright was infringed" 17 U.S.C. §§ 502-505

Glossary of Infringement Remedies

"*Injunctions:* An injunction" https://www.law.cornell.edu/wex/injunction

"In copyright actions, federal courts" *Antioch Co., v. Scrapbook Borders, Inc.,* 292 F. Supp. 980 (2003)

"*Copyright Owners Actual Damages:* Damages are" https://www.law.cornell.edu/we/damages

"*Statutory Damages:* Statutory damages are the most common" *Copyright Fundamentals,* LEXIS Practical Guidance Note, maintained by

"If your copyright was registered before" 17 U.S.C.§§ 412, 505

"Statutory damage awards typically range" Lex Machina®, *Copyright and Trademark Litigation Report 2021.* Available at: https://pages.lexmachina.com/2021-Copyright-Trademark-Report_LP.html

"*Attorneys Fees and Costs:* A court may order" 17 U.S.C. §505

"*Impoundment and Destruction:* The Copyright Act provides" 17 U.S.C. §503

"The average cost of litigation" Report from American Intellectual Property Law Association (AIPLA), 2019 Report of the Economic Survey, at I-208 (2019); Available at:https://www.aipla.org/detail/journal-issue/2019-report-of-the-economic-survey

The CASE Act

"On an individual level" Copyright Small Claims, *A Report of the Registrar of Copyrights,* September 2013 or 2018

"The Copyright Alternative in Small-Claims Enforcement Act of 2019" " 17 U.S.C. §§1501-1511

There are Limitations

"The CCB can award statutory damages of $15,000.00 per work" 17 U.S.C. §1504

It is All Volunteer

"No one can be compelled to take part in a CCB proceeding " 17 U.S.C. §1506 (i)

Benefits of CCB Proceeding

"*DIY Resolutions:* The simpler, streamlined procedures" 17 U.S.C. §1506 (d)

"*Eliminates costly travel:* 17 U.S.C. §§1506 (c) (1)

"*Registration Relief:* You can start" 17 U.S.C.§1501 (c) (1)

"*Guidance:* The CCB will make available" www.ccb.gov

The Digital Millenium Copyright Act

"In 1998, the Digital Millenium Copyright Act" 17 U.S.C. §§512, 1201, 1202

Safe Harbors

"A safe harbor is a legal provision" https://www.law.cornell.edu/wex/safeharbor

"In exchange for " 17 U.S.C. §512

"The DMCA, like all copyright law, is territorial." https://www.copyright.gov/512/ Frequently Asked Questions

"These are the steps" https://www.copyright.gov/512/

Step 1 The Take-Down Notice

"Takedown notices should include the following information

"Many online service providers, like Facebook

"When the ISP (or OSP) receives a take-down notice" 17 U.S.C.§512(g)

Step 3 Counter Notices

"The last item can be a game changer" *Epic Games , Inc., v. Mendes,*2018 U.S> Dist LEXIS 14954 (N.D.Cal. 2018)

"A counter-notice essentially says" https://www.copyright.gov/512/sample-counter-notice.pdf

Ten Day Window

"If a valid counter-notice " 17 U.S.C § 512(2)(c)

Anti-Circumvention

"These provisions make it illegal" " 17 U.S.C § 1201

"It is also illegal to remove" " 17 U.S.C §1202

There are (Evolving) Exemptions

"Library browsing" " 17 U.S.C §1202(d) "

"Every three years" " 17 U.S.C §1201(A)(1)(c)

"The current exemption list" 37 C.F.R. §201.40

There are Serious Consequences

"On the civil side" " 17 U.S.C § 1203

"Fines of up to $500,000.00" " 17 U.S.C §1203

Table of Illustrations

Cover: *Idea Expression Divide Diptych* by Deborah Reid © 2018
Page 6: Introductory Materials frontispiece: *Open Book* by Deborah Reid © 2022
Page 8: *Algorithm* by Deborah Reid © 2021
Page 9: *Hart of the Night* by Mary Atwood © 2021
Page 10: *Public Enrichment* by Deborah Reid © 2015
Page 11: *Story* by Deborah Reid © 2019
Page 12: *Copyright Triptych* by Deborah Reid © 2022
Page 13: U.S. Constitution
Page 14: U.S. Courts Map
Page 15: Mary's website on Mary's laptop
Page 16: Subject Matter frontispiece: *Target Copyright* by Deborah Reid © 2017
Page 18: Queen Anne and the Statute of Anne
Page 19: *Our Overworked Supreme Court* by J. Keppler, 1885
Page 20: *Oscar Wilde No. 18* by Napoleon Sarony
Page 21: *Tango* by Deborah Reid © 2019
Page 21: *The Laughing Cavalier* by Frans Hals
Page 22: *Fixation Trio* by Mary Atwood © 2022
Page 23: *Standout* by Mary Atwood © 2022
Page 24: *Lost Thoughts* by Mary Atwood © 2022
Page 25: *Tools of the Trade* by Mary Atwood © 2022
Page 26: *Wallace Shows* posters by George Bleistein
Page 27: *Under the Big Top* by Mary Atwood © 2018
Page 28: *Universe of Intellectual Property* by Deborah Reid © 2016
Page 29: Symbol, Motto, Packaging examples
Page 30: *Shhh* by Mary Atwood © 2020
Page 31: *Pause* by Deborah Reid © 2020
Page 32: *Idea Expression Divide Diptych* by Deborah Reid © 2018
Page 33: *Relativity* by Deborah Reid © 2018
Page 33: *Think About It, Rodin* by Mary Atwood © 2013
Page 34: *Blurry* by Deborah Reid © 2019
Page 34: *Absent* by Mary Atwood © 2013
Page 35: Case Exhibits: Kaplan v Stock Market Photo Agency
Page 36: Case Exhibits: Direct Marketing of Va, v. E.Mishan & Sons, Inc.
Page 36: Case Exhibits: Kerr v. New Yorker Magazine
Page 37: Mary and her Mother, Deborah and her Mother
Page 38: *Facts* by Deborah Reid © 2022
Page 39: *Feeling Froggy* by Mary Atwood © 2010
Page 40: *First Reading of the Emancipation Proclamation of President Lincoln* by Francis Bicknell Carpenter
Page 42: *Discovering Dannon* by Mary Atwood © 2024
Page 43: *Yee Haw* by Mary Atwood © 2022
Page 44: *Useful Things* by Deborah Reid © 2019
Page 44: Reglor Lamps catalog page
Page 45: Case Exhibits: Varsity Brands v Star Athletica
Page 46: Case Exhibits: Design Idea v Meijer

Page 47: *ABC, No ©* by Deborah Reid © 2023
Page 48: *Everything is Possible* by Mary Atwood © 2013
Page 49: Geometric Shapes
Page 49: Geometric Shapes incorporated into designs
Page 50: Colors and Coloration as used in fabric designs
Page 50: *Watercolor World* by Mary Atwood © 2022
Page 51: Digitally altered photograph
Page 52: *Contrasting Sounds* by Wassily Kandinsky
Page 52: *Lavender Liberty* by Mary Atwood © 2021
Page 53: *The Public Domain Pool* by Deborah Reid © 2023
Page 56: Exclusive Rights frontispiece: *Bundle of Rights* by Deborah Reid © 2019
Page 58: *Bundle of Rights* by Deborah Reid © 2019
Page 59: *Small Bundle* by Deborah Reid © 2017
Page 59: *Send Love* by Deborah Reid © 2020
Page 60: *French Umbrella* by Deborah Reid © 2013
Page 61: *Rights Triptych* by Deborah Reid © 2022
Page 62: *Flower Times Flower* by Deborah Reid © 2022
Page 63: *Victrola* by Mary Atwood © 2023
Page 66: *Timeless* by Mary Atwood © 2021
Page 67: *Read Happy Tapir* by Deborah Reid © 2023
Page 68: *Shades of Gray with Butterfly* by Mary Atwood and Deborah Reid © 2021
Page 69: *Sequels* by Mary Atwood © 2022
Page 70: *CX2* by Deborah Reid © 2023
Page 71: *A Moment* by Deborah Reid © 2023
Page 72: *Send Love Triptych* by Deborah Reid © 2022
Page 73: *Yes, but Be Careful* by Mary Atwood © 2022
Page 74: *Creative Expression* by Deborah Reid © 2023
Page 76: *The Careless Dancer* by Mary Atwood © 2010
Page 77: *Peking Duck* by Mary Atwood © 2009
Page 81: *The Long Room* by Deborah Reid © 2022
Page 82: *Money Makes the World Go Round* by Mary Atwood © 2018
Page 83: *Bargain Books* by Mary Atwood © 2023
Page 84: *Sotheby's* by Deborah Reid © 2019
Page 85: *Blockchain Ledger* by Deborah Reid © 2021
Page 86: *Our Lady of Paris* by Mary Atwood © 2018
Page 87: *Phoenix Art District* by Mary Atwood © 2023
Page 88: Ownership Frontispiece: *Pie in the Sky* by Deborah Reid © 2022
Page 90: *Algorithm Trio* by Deborah Reid © 2023
Page 91: Statute of Anne
Page 92: *Pseudonymous Women* by Mary Atwood © 2022
Page 93: *Liberty Survives* by Mary Atwood © 2009
Page 94: *Copy Cat* by Mary Atwood © 2022
Page 95: *Robotic Sketch* by Mary Atwood © 2018
Page 96: *Zarya of the Dawn* cover
Page 97: *Zarya of the Dawn illustrations*, text, and selection example
Page 98: *Edmond de Belamy, from La Famille de Belamy* by Obvious
Page 101: *Collaborate* by Deborah Reid © 2023

Page 101: *Camille Claudel and Auguste Rodin by* Studio Cesar, Paris, and George Charles Beresford, respectively
Page 103: *Judging the Spawn* by Mary Atwood © 2023
Page 105: *Royalty is Different* by Mary Atwood © 2018
Page 106: *1 or 2* by Deborah Reid © 2022
Page 107: *Heart of Stone* by Mary Atwood © 2022
Page 109: *7 Q* by Mary Atwood © 2023
Page 112: *Pandemic Plate* by Deborah Reid © 2020
Page 115: *Creative Commons Logo* by Shepard Fairey © 2010
Page 118: Fair Use frontispiece: *The Four Factors* by Deborah Reid © 2019
Page 120: *Philip Yorke, 1st Earl of Hardwicke* by Michael Dahl
Page 121: *The Athenaeum Portrait* by Gilbert Stuart
Page 123: *Pretty, Hairy, Big, Bald Headed, Two Timing Woman* by Deborah Reid © 2019
Page 124: *Parisian Love Locks* by Mary Atwood © 2012
Page 125: *Puzzles* by Deborah Reid © 2020
Page 127: *The Four Factors* by Deborah Reid © 2019
Page 128: *The Weight* by Mary Atwood and Deborah Reid © 2023
Page 128: *Blurry* by Deborah Reid © 2019
Page 129: *Factor 1* by Deborah Reid © 2019
Page 130: *Money on the Table* by Deborah Reid © 2019
Page 131: Case Exhibits: Goldsmith v Warhol
Page 132: Case Exhibits: Goldsmith v Warhol
Page 135: Case Exhibits Blanch v Koons
Page 136: *Factor 2* by Deborah Reid © 2019
Page 136: *Core Strength* by Deborah Reid © 2019
Page 138: *Factor 3* by Deborah Reid © 2019
Page 139: Gerald Ford Autobiography cover and The Nation logo
Page 140: Case Exhibits: Bill Graham Archives v Dorling Kindersley, Ltd.
Page 141: *Factor 4* by Deborah Reid © 2019
Page 141: Case Exhibits: Schwartzwald v Oath, Inc.
Page 143: *Critical* by Deborah Reid © 2022
Page 144: *Interrelated Question* by Deborah Reid © 2022
Page 145: Case Exhibit: Brammer v. Violent Hues Productions
Page 145: Case Exhibits: Rogers v. Koons
Page 146: Case Exhibit: Noland v. Janssen
Page 146: Case Exhibit: Konangataa v. Am. Broadcasting Companies, Inc.
Page 148: Legal Care and Protection frontispiece: *Tools* by Deborah Reid © 2019
Page 151: Form VA, Page 1 and Certificate of Registration
Page 153: Form VA
Page 157: *Library of Congress* by Deborah Reid © *2016*
Page 158: *Annotated Bundle of Rights* by Deborah Reid © 2022
Page 159: *Mary on Mary* by Deborah Reid © 2022
Page 160: Case Exhibit: Harney v. Sony Pictures
Page 166: The maximum amount the Copyright Claims Board can award
Page 168: *Sunset Harbor* by Mary Atwood © 2022
Page 169: *Blue Door Steps* by Mary Atwood © 2023
Page 173: *The End* by Deborah Reid and Mary Atwood © 2022

INDEX

1st Circuit, 159
2 Live Crew, 123, 137
2nd Circuit, 14, 63, 87, 103, 132, 135, 140
5 Pointz, 87
7 Questions, 110
7th Circuit, 23, 43, 103
9th Circuit, 14, 69, 72, 73, 84, 94, 103
11th Circuit, 114

A

Account books, 54
Abramovic, Marina, 101
Act for the Encouragement of Learning, 18, 91
Acuff-Rose Music, Inc., 123
Affirmative defense, 126
AI, 95-100, 154
Alcott, Louisa May, 92
Algorithm, 95-99
Alphabet, 28, 47, 52
Amount and substantiality used, 100, 121
Andy Warhol Foundation, 125, 130-131
Animal(s), 94
Anti-circumvention, 168, 172
Antenna, 77
Antioch Company, 67
Apple iTunes, 63, 83
Architectural work(s), 25, 72, 90, 153
Artificial intelligence, 95-100, 154
Assignment(s), 111-113
Audiovisual work(s), 25, 72, 76, 110
Author(s), 10-13, 18-20, 22, 26, 33, 37-42, 53, 58-60, 62, 64, 66, 68, 74, 76, 83, 90-105, 107-109, 111, 115, 121, 122, 129, 134, 137, 142, 151, 152
Authorship, 13, 19, 20, 38, 42, 86, 90, 96, 98, 99, 102, 104, 122
Automat, 24

B

Bad faith, 130, 135
Baker, W. C. M., 34
Banksy, 87
Barbour, Judy, 43
Basquiat, Jean-Michel, 85
Beatles, The, 101
Benesh Dance Notation, 22
Blanch, Andrea, 134-135, 137
Bleistein principle, 27-27
Boden, Margaret O.B.E., FBA, 95
Brammer, Russell, 145
Bright lines, 34, 128, 134
Bronte, Anne, Charlotte, Emily, 92
Buchel, Christoph, 74-75
Building blocks of language, 47
Burrow-Giles, 20, 97
Bundle of rights, 12, 58, 59, 61, 62, 71, 81, 90, 158

C

Cache page(s), 64
Calligraphy, 47
Campbell, Luther R., 123
Carroll, Anna Ella, 40-41
Cartoon character(s), 29, 70
CASE Act, 166
Category of work, 25
Caveat creator, 8, 55
Cease and desist, 162
Certiorari, writ of, 15
Chicago, Judy, 41
Chicago Park District, 23
Choreographic work(s), 22, 25, 72
Charitable, 78
Cheerleading uniform(s), 45, 47
Christo, 87, 101
Circus poster(s), 26
Citizenship, 93
Civil law, 24, 86
Claudel, Camille, 101
Close, Chuck, 84

Co-author(s), 9, 99, 101-105
Coca Cola, 30
Collaboration, 12, 90, 101
Collective work(s), 42, 110, 154
Colors and coloration, 50-51
Coloring book, 50
Commentary, 43, 121, 122, 130, 133, 139
Commercial use, 85, 100, 116, 123, 127, 129, 130, 132, 133
Commercial work(s), 28-29, 100, 134, 141
Comic book, 92, 101, 103-104
Commission, 90, 101, 103-111, 130, 134, 154
Community for Creative Non-Violence, 107
Compilation(s), 42-43, 101
Computer program(s), 25, 47, 124, 137
Contribution, 102-104, 108, 110, 154, 156
Cookbook(s), 42-43
Co-owner(s), 101-102, 104
Constitution, U.S., 13, 19, 22, 52, 58, 91, 121
Copy, 62-65, 71, 80, 81, 84, 95, 113, 152, 159, 172
Copyleft, 115
Copyrightable, 14, 35, 37-39, 45, 47, 49-51, 61, 69, 78, 91, 93, 102-104, 124, 129, 139, 158, 159
Copyright Act of 1976, 14, 58, 59, 76, 121, 126
Copyright Claims Board, 151, 166
Copyright Clause, 13, 19, 22
Copyright Notice, 12, 44, 150, 154, 172
Coqui, 39
Counter-notice, 170-171
Cowboy Chow, 43
Creation, 13, 21, 38, 53, 59, 63, 71, 90-92, 109, 116, 122, 129, 132, 137,

151, 154
Creative Commons, 115-117
Creative expression, 19, 43, 49, 76, 136
Creativity, 37, 38, 51, 58, 59, 96, 98, 115, 122
Criticism, 126, 129, 130, 133, 143

D
Duke Nukem, **69**
de Koonig, Elaine, 92
Dentist, 21
Deposit copies, 157
Deposit, mandatory, 157
Derivative work(s), 12, 59, 61, 66-70, 85, 99, 104-105, 116, 132-134, 142-143, 145, 159
Design Ideas, Ltd., 46
Design patent(s), 30
Digital Millenium Copyright Act, 14, 168-171
Dill, Laddie John, 84
The Dinner Party, 40-41
Disclaimer, 8
Discover Dannon, 42-43
Display right, 71-75, 76
Distribution, public, 80
Distribution right, 79-81, 83
DMCA Take Down Notice, 12, 70, 169
Donaldson Lithographing, 26
Dramatic work(s), 25
Droit moral, 86
Dynamic, 24, 58, 59

E
Ecclesiastes 1:9, 66
Educational purpose, 100, 127, 129
Effect of the use, 100, 127, 141
Eliot, George, 92
Employee, 31, 106-107, 110
Employment, scope of, 106, 110, 154
The Empty Chair, 40
Exclusive rights, 12, 13, 22, 58, 60, 61, 65, 78, 81, 84, 85, 90, 104, 111, 151, 158

Exemption(s), 65, 68, 72, 75, 78, 172
Exportation, 82
Expression
    Creative, 19, 43, 49, 76, 136
    Medium of, 19, 90

F
Fact(s), 38-43
Fairey, Shepard, 115
Factors, fair use, 12, 100, 120-147
Fair abridgement, 121
Fair Use, 12, 13, 14, 61, 64, 65, 68, 70,72, 96, 99, 100, 120-147
Fan art and fan fiction, 70
Federal courts, 14, 44, 164, 166
Federal statutes, 14
Fee(s), 99, 152, 155, 163, 164, 172
Fiction, 41, 70, 137
First Amendment, 13, 27, 80, 139
First factor, 127, 129-135
First publication, 80, 150
First sale doctrine, 65, 83-84
Fixation 13, 19, 22-25, 90
Fixed, 19, 22, 45, 46, 48, 62, 80, 154, 159
Folsom, Wells and Thurston, 121
Font(s), 47
Ford, Gerald R., 80, 139
Forms, TX, VA SE, PA, etc., 153, 169
Forrest, Katherine B., J., 73
Fourth factor, 127, 141-143

G
Garden, 23
Geometric shape(s), 49
Gerhartsreiter, Christian Karl, 160
Goldman, Jason, 73
Goldsmith, Lynn, 125, 130-132
Google, 72, 124-125, 139, 168
Gaiman, Neal, 103-104
Graffit, 48
Graham, Bill, 140
Graphic work(s), 19, 22, 45, 76, 85, 140, 143
Grateful Dead, 140

Greenbie, Marjorie Barstow, 40-41
Guitar(s), 67
Gurry, Frances, 59
Gutenberg, Johann, 18, 120
Gyles v. Wilcox, 120

H
Hals, Frans, 21
Hamm, Jon, 141-142
Hand, Learned. J., 33
Harney, Donald A., 160-161
Harper & Row, 80, 139
Hardwicke, Lord, 120
History, 18, 40, 71, 79, 92
Holmes, Oliver Wendell, J., 26
Human, 95-99, 154

I
Idea/expression divide, 14, 32-36
Idea(s), 10, 19, 28, 33, 34, 43, 46, 52, 122
Implication, license by, 113
Indentiko, Inc., 39
Independent contractor, 106
Industrial design, 30
Infringement, 12, 20, 21, 26, 34-37, 39, 40, 41, 42, 45, 58, 61, 66-69, 70, 72, 73, 77, 78, 83, 94, 99, 120-123, 126, 132, 135, 137, 139, 140, 143, 158-165, 166, 168, 169, 170
Instructional text, 108, 110, 154
Intellectual property, 18, 28, 30, 52, 53, 70, 75, 93, 105, 108, 111
Intent, 102, 153, 158
Internet, 13, 15, 43, 59, 77, 167, 169
Internet treaties, 59-60
Invention, 18, 24, 30, 58

J
Java, 124
Jeane-Claude, 101
Jellyfish, 39
Jesse, Jim, 78
Joint author(s), 102, 104, 105
Joint works, 101, 102, 104, 105

K
Kaplan, Peter B., 35

Kapoor, Anish, 51
Kashtanova, Kristina, 96
Kelley, Chapman, 23
Kerr, Thomas, 36
Koons, Jeff, 134-135, 137, 145
Kunz, Anita, 36

L

Labanotation, 22
Lawsuit, 14, 40, 43, 68, 70, 99, 101, 163-165
Laysiepen, Ula, 101
Learned men, 91, 92
Leval, Pierre N., J., 122
Libraries, 65, 83
Library of Congress, 157, 172
License, 51, 61, 66, 85, 99, 109, 112-117, 123, 131, 164
Limitation(s), 65, 68, 75, 78, 82, 115, 126, 154, 156, 165, 166
Links, 8, 11, 54
Literary work(s), 19, 25, 62, 65, 82
Logos, 29, 133, 153
London Sire, 79-80
Lowry, Christophe, 39

M

Machine(s), 95, 108
Makeup, 22
Making available right, 60
Mandatory deposit, 157
Map(s) and chart(s), 25, 121
Marsh, Capen and Lyon, 121
Market impact, 99, 100, 121, 142-143, 164
Mashable, 73
MASS MoCA, 74-75
Materiality, 80
McFarlane, Todd, 103-104
Medieval Spawn, 103-104
Medium
    of expression, 19, 90
    Tangible, 19, 45, 46, 80, 90, 159
Midjourney, 95-98
Meijer, Inc., 46

Mickey Mouse, 29, 53, 54
Miller, Lee, 101
Mills, June Tarpé, 92
Monopoly, 10, 29, 33, 39, 43, 51, 52, 86, 122
Moral rights, 86
Motion picture work(s), 22, 108, 110, 137, 154
Mourabit, Sammy, 22
Museum collections, 54

N

Napster, 81
Nars, Francisco, 22
Naruto, 94
Nasty Woman, 123, 137
Nation, The, 80, 139
Nature of the copyrighted work, 100, 127, 136
Niagara, 134-135, 137
Nixon, Richard M., 80, 139
NFT, 85
No bright lines, 34, 128, 134
Noland, Cady, 146
Non-profit educational purpose, 129
Notice, 12, 44, 70, 87, 150, 154, 157, 168-170, 172

O

Obvious (Art), 98
Oh, the Places You'll Go!, 142-143
Oh, Pretty Woman, 123, 137
Oracle, 124
Orbison, Roy, 123, 137
Original, 19, 20, 28, 38, 39, 40, 42, 63, 68, 70, 81, 84, 85, 90, 104, 108, 121, 123, 125, 129-134, 138, 140, 145, 150, 158-161
Originality, 12, 19-21, 25, 38, 41, 90, 103
Ossenmacher, Joel, 63

P

Packaging, 29
Pantomime(s), 22, 25, 76
Paparazzi, 142
Parody, 123, 129, 137

Patents, 28, 30, 44
PETA, 94
Perfect 10, 72
Performance art, 24
Performance right, 61, 76-77
Performance rights organization(s), 61, 78
Phonorecord(s), 61, 62-64, 79-81, 126, 157
Photography, 19, 20-22, 25, 62, 66, 72-74, 80, 83, 86, 91, 94, 96, 111, 114, 125, 130-135, 137, 141-142, 145, 150, 153, 155, 156, 160-161, 172
Pickett, Ferdinand, 67-68
Pictorial work(s), 26, 35, 45, 67, 108
Pohl, Mitchell, DDS, 21
Potter, Harry, 69, 92
Prince, 67-68, 125, 130-133
Printing press, 18, 58, 120
Print, historical, 25
Privacy, right of, 28
Pseudonym, 92
Public performance, 12, 60, 77, 78
Publicity, right of, 28
Published, 34., 37, 42, 43, 80, 91, 93, 94, 120-122, 130, 134, 136, 139, 140, 153-157, 160
Published photograph(s), 153, 155, 156
Public domain, 12, 18, 21, 37, 39, 47, 52-55, 115, 159
Purpose and character of use, 100, 121, 125, 127, 129, 131, 133, 140, 141, 145
Purpose of copyright, 10, 34, 124

Q

R

RAM, 64
Ray, Man, 101
Readers Digest, 80
ReDigi, 63, 83
Rehyer, Rebecca, 37
Reglor of California, 44

Registration, 12, 93, 95, 96, 98, 151-157, 159, 162, 167, 169
Reid, James Earl, 107
Remedies, 12, 163
Reproduction right, 62, 65, 71
Resale royalties, 84, 85
Rockefeller, Clark, 160
Rodriguez-Miranda, Angel Edgardo, 39
Rogers, Art, 145
Rogers and Hammerstein, 101
Royalties, 84, 85, 103, 105
Rudolph, Larry, 63

S

Safe harbor, 155, 168, 170, 171
Sarony, Napolean, 20, 21
Satava, Richard, 39
Scope of employment, 106, 110, 154
Scrapbook Borders, 67
Schwartzwald, Lawrence, 141, 142
Scènes à faire, 37
Scholarship, 126, 129, 139
Sculpture, 13, 22, 28, 39, 46, 51, 66, 76, 83, 85, 86, 87, 90, 91, 107, 145, 146, 150, 154, 157
Sculptural work(s), 25
Second factor, 124, 127, 136-137
Selden, Charles, 34
Semple, Stewart, 51
Sequel, 69, 70, 133
Server test, 72-73
Sesame Street, 37
Simon and Garfunkel, 101
Singularity Black, 51
Seuss, Dr., 142-143
Sinclair, Stephanie 73-74
Silk Stockings, 134-135
Slater, David, 94
Slogans, 28-29
Small claims, 12, 151, 159
Social bargain, 10, 59-60
Sonny Bono Copyright Term Extension Act, 53
Sotheby's, 84

Spawn, 103-104
Star Athletica, 45-47
Statute of Anne 18, 120
Statutes, 11, 14
Steamboat Willie, 53
Stickers, 67
Stock Market Photo Agency, 35
Stories, 11, 34, 37, 69, 108, 126, 145
Story, Joseph, Jr., J., 121
Street art, 48, 87
Subject matter, 12, 16-55, 91
Substantiality, 100, 121, 127, 138, 139
Supplementary works, 108, 110, 154
Symbol(s), 28, 29, 47, 67-68

T

Take down notice, 12, 70, 162, 169
Tangible medium, 19, 45, 46, 80, 90, 159
Term 19, 30, 42, 48, 52, 53, 66, 86, 106, 109
Term of Art, 18, 22, 29, 63, 80
Territorial, 13
Test(s), 46, 72-73, 108, 110, 154, 156, 159
    Answer material for, 108, 110, 154
Teter, Lee, 62-63
Title(s), slogan(s), and motto(s), 28-29
Theory, 52
Third factor, 127, 138-140
Threshold requirement(s), 12, 19-24, 25, 90
Tiffany, 29
Trademark(s), 29
Trade secret(s), 30-31
Transfers, 81, 111
Transformative, 100, 122, 130, 133-135, 142
Transformativeness, 132-133
Transmit clause, 76-78
Translation, 110
Treaties, 14, 59-60, 93

Typeface, 47

U

Umbrella solution, 60
Useful article(s), 19, 30, 44-46, 124
U.S. Constitution 13, 22, 58, 91
U.S. Court of Appeals, 14
U.S. District Court(s), 14, 70, 98, 122
U.S. government publication(s), 28
Unpublished, 53, 93, 153-156
Unpublished photograph(s), 153-156
Utilitarian object(s), 28, 44-46

V

Van Bruggen, Coosje, 101
VARA, 86-87, 109
Varsity Brands, 45-47
Vessel hull(s), 25
Violent Hues Productions, 145
Visual Artists Rights Act, 86-87

W

W Magazine, 22
Warhol, Andy, 11, 101, 125, 130-134
Washington, George, 121
Weighed together, 144
Wilde, Oscar, 11, 20, 21
Wildflower Works, 23
WIPO, 59, 172
WIPO Copyright Treaty, 59, 172
WIPO Performances and Phonograms Treaty, 59
Wolfe, Tom, 24
Wood, Kimba, J., 73
World Intellectual Property Organization, 59
Writings, 13, 19, 58, 85, 91, 121
Works made for hire, 12, 106, 109, 110, 154

X

Y

Yorke, Philip, 1st Earl of Hardwicke, 120

Z

Zarya of the Dawn, 96-68

ABOUT THE AUTHORS

Deborah Reid is a lifelong artist and an attorney with four decades of experience. She is a graduate of the University of San Diego School of Law, and a member of the bars of California, Florida and New York.

Reid is passionate about sharing her legal knowledge and educating other creatives about their rights. She combines analytical and artistic skills to create striking visual illustrations and clear explanations of legal concepts. Her legal reference guides, seminars and lectures are vibrant and informative.

Photograph by Tiffany Manning

Mary Atwood is an award winning photographer and the author of *Historic Homes of Florida's First Coast*.

Atwood's photographs have been included in numerous corporate and private collections, and have been exhibited in museums, galleries, and public art venues. Most notably, Mary was selected by the Sister Cities Committee of Nantes, France to exhibit her *"First Coast Reflections"* project as part of the inaugural celebration for "la Maison des Etates-Unis" in 2013. To date, her work has won more than fifty awards in local, regional, and national juried exhibitions.

Photograph by Tiffany Manning

Deborah and Mary are available for in person or virtual lectures and seminars on copyright law. For additional information, please contact Deborah at reidartlaw.com/learning.

NOTES